Reconciling Embrace

Foundations

for the

Future of

Sacramental

Reconciliation

D1470245

Reconciling Embrace

Foundations

for the

Future of

Sacramental

Reconciliation

Robert J. Kennedy

Editor

LITURGY
TRAINING
PUBLICATIONS

Acknowledgments

The excerpt from Toni Morrison's *Beloved* was reprinted by permission of International Creative Management, Inc. Copyright © 1987 by Alfred A. Knopf.

Margaret M. Mitchell's chapter "Paul's 1 Corinthians on Reconciliation in the Church: Promise and Pitfalls" first appeared in the May 1997 issue of *New Theology Review* and is reprinted here with permission.

This book was edited by Robert J. Kennedy with assistance from Victoria Tufano. Deborah Bogaert was the production editor. The book was designed by Kristyn Kalnes and set in Caslon and Nueva by Jim Mellody-Pizzato. Cover photo by Antonio Pérez. Printed by Versa Press of East Peoria, Illinois.

Copyright © 1998, Archdiocese of Chicago: Liturgy Training Publications, 1800 North Hermitage Avenue, Chicago IL 60622-1101; 1-800-933-1800; fax 1-800-933-7094. All rights reserved.

02 01 00 99 98   5 4 3 2 1

Library of Congress Catalog Card Number: 98-65603

SYMREC

In Memory of

James B. Dunning

Passionate and Prophetic

Evangelist of Reconciliation

in Christ

1937 – 1995

Contents

Introduction

Robert J. Kennedy

Since the mid-1980s, as a development of its work in Christian initiation, the North American Forum on the Catechumenate (Forum) has promoted the work of reconciliation by offering ReMembering Church institutes throughout the United States and Canada. ReMembering Church, a parish-based, sacramental ministry with inactive and alienated Catholics who are in the process of returning to the church, is modeled on the process of the *Rite of Christian Initiation of Adults* and is faithful to the penitential process outlined in the *Rite of Penance* (paragraphs 6 and 20).

The roots of ReMembering Church can be traced to two sources. The first is a proposal by the late Cardinal Joseph Bernardin of Chicago at the 1983 Synod of Bishops for "a fourth form for the *Rite of Penance*," based on the model of the *Rite of Christian Initiation of Adults* and for use in the pastoral care of returning Catholics.[1] The second is James Lopresti's work and study in the early 1980s on conversion and initiation, and his critical research on what the journey of return would look like. Based on his work in initiation, Lopresti knew that the dynamics of the initiation process — celebrating the journey of conversion ritually — needed to be an integral part of any Catholic Christian journey. Thus, ReMembering Church was born.[2]

Forum's ReMembering Church institutes provide training for pastoral ministers who want to deepen their understanding of reconciling alienated and inactive Catholics. Participants explore their own experience of alienation and reconciliation, and reflect on the implications of these experiences for their ministry among those who are estranged from the church. A team of facilitators/presenters offers theological, psychological and pastoral information, strategies for parish implementation and rituals for celebration.

Unlike initiation, however, the process of reconciling returning Catholics has no ritual steps designated and mandated by the church. The introduction to the *Rite of Penance* (paragraphs 1 – 40) provides a theological foundation for the celebration of reconciliation of alienated Catholics, but it does not address the process and issues of return in a larger ministerial context. By providing the vision of process and formation from the *Rite of Christian Initiation of Adults*, ReMembering Church makes its greatest contribution to the life and ministry of the church.

Pastoral ministers who participate in these ReMembering Church institutes are excited by the vision and the possibilities discovered in them, and many have experienced a good degree of success as they have integrated this reconciliation process into the flow of parish ministry.[3] Yet many theological and pastoral questions have arisen. What are the nature and dynamics of reconciliation? How can ReMembering Church be adapted to the variety of circumstances people find themselves in as they seek to return to the church? Reconciliation is a human as well as an ecclesial phenomenon: How do we as church address this range of human experience?

Funded by a grant from an anonymous donor, Forum, in cooperation with Catholic Theological Union in Chicago, was able to sponsor *To Forgive, To Heal, To Liberate: A Symposium on Reconciliation and ReMembering Church*, in April 1995. This interdisciplinary meeting brought together 44 participants: experts from a variety of disciplines, team members from ReMembering Church institutes, and key leadership persons in the fields of reconciliation, evangelization, liturgy, ministry and small Christian communities. The purpose was to engage the human sciences (sociology, psychology, anthropology) and the Christian tradition (social ethics, scripture, history and sacramental theology) in substantial and critical reflection on the pastoral issues of reconciliation.

This volume makes available to a wider audience the seven major presentations of the symposium. Keynote speaker and social ethicist Toinette Eugene, associate professor of Christian social ethics at Garrett Evangelical Theological Seminary at the time of the symposium and a noted lecturer, author and editor in the areas of social ethics, theology in a global context and feminist/womanist theology, sets the symposium's conversation firmly in the social, communal context of today's church and world. Does reconciliation have a future, she asks, in a church and world so deeply divided and dislocated by pervasive forms of social and individual sin?

Sociologist James Davidson of Purdue University draws a profile of alienation in the Catholic Church today from the findings of the recently completed Catholic Pluralism Project.

Paul Philibert, OP, of the University of Notre Dame, explores from the viewpoint of pastoral psychology the relationships among childhood psychosocial development, moral experience, spiritual maturity and ritual.

Anthropologist Fredric Roberts of Michigan State University raises provocative questions about pastoral and theological methodologies as he compares anthropologists with liturgists and pastoral ministers. He asks: Do we have an honest knowledge of our assumptions and biases as we enter, attend to and report the world of others? Can we open ourselves and be vulnerable enough to hear others honestly tell their stories? These are necessary "pre-questions" for the ministry of reconciliation.

New Testament professor Margaret Mitchell of McCormick Theological Seminary raises up the promises and pitfalls of reconciliation in seven arguments Paul makes in his First Letter to the Corinthians; how we will be church is the fundamental practical issue for us, as it was for the Corinthians.

Theologian and historian James Dallen of Gonzaga University opens up the storehouse of the church's tradition of penance to reveal the variety of its forms and their characteristic features. This variety tells a story of change in the church's penitential and reconciling practices according to the needs of Christians.

Finally, theologian and liturgist Kathleen Hughes, RSCJ, of Catholic Theological Union, calls us to revisit the introduction to the *Rite of Penance* with renewed and deep study in order to find theological perspectives that will ground the future development of penance and reconciliation.

This book is meant to include its readers in the conversation that the symposium began. These stimulating essays from an interdisciplinary "panel of experts" open good, fertile ground from which good pastoral practice can grow. To bring the readers in on the conversation then, each essay is followed by a brief section titled "For Pastoral Reflection and Response." These are, in most cases, based on responses given by various people at the meeting; those individuals are credited in the responses. The comments and questions raised are meant to stimulate reflection on the present pastoral and liturgical life of the church for the sake of creative practical strategies of reconciliation. As Dr. Eugene reminds us, our time and situation require a fertile and faith-formed imagination in order to proclaim the Christian message of reconciliation.

No human enterprise, including the preparation of a book, is ever done in isolation. So I thank from the bottom of my heart the seven presenters whose thoughtful and provocative talks now take shape as the essays in this book; the twelve participants who prepared and delivered the responses that serve as the basis for the pastoral reflections of this book; and all the participants at the symposium whose passionate and articulate engagement in the discussion bodes well for the future of reconciliation. I am also deeply grateful to Alice Prattico, without whose word processing skills this book would never have seen the light of day, and to Vicky Tufano of Liturgy Training Publications, who waited with patience and good humor until it did.

I am most grateful to Thomas Morris, the executive director of the North American Forum on the Catechumenate. Not only did he provide for all the details that supported the original symposium, from applying for the grant to videotaping the sessions, but he also provided, and continues to provide, steady, faith-filled support and a caring, critical eye for Forum's work of reconciliation. These are welcome gifts for this ministry.

Reconciliation in the Pastoral Context of Today's Church and World
Does Reconciliation Have a Future?

Toinette M. Eugene

Does reconciliation have a future? In the pastoral context of today's church and world, does reconciliation have a future? We dare to raise these open-ended, wide-ranging questions in the aftermath of a terrorist attack in Oklahoma City that evoked the social sin of racism in the form of the anger of the nation. The fear and frustration resulting from the atrocity had been projected and extended, with worldwide and warmongering implications, to persons of Middle Eastern and Arabic heritage and social location until we discovered that the evil and the sinfulness emerged from within our own borders.[1] We must raise the question, Does reconciliation have a future in relationship to the social as well as personal sins of racism, so defined by the United States Bishops' Pastoral Letter *Brothers and Sisters to Us: On Racism in Our Day*?[2]

We have felt the painful memories rekindled in the remembrance of a renowned world statesman, former Secretary of Defense Robert McNamara, in a retrospective remorse over his part in the sin of militarism committed by the leaders of our nation in the destruction of Vietnam.[3] We long for social as well as personal reconciliation with our enemies and oppressors because of our evolving roles in public or personal conflict, as it may be observed and seen in our tradition of moving forward from an emphasis on "just war" theories to magisterial Catholic social teachings that focus primarily on the gospel of peace and justice.[4]

There is one final social and personal context to which I must aver and which I will utilize as a paradigm for our exploration of a future for reconciliation in the church and world. Does reconciliation have a future in the pastoral context of today's church and world as we reflect on the reality of the sin of sexism and its implications for women? Does reconciliation have a future for abused, economically disenfranchised women or seemingly ecclesially "abandoned" and disrespected women who, as images of Mother Church, have served, have saved, have nurtured and sustained men and children, and have led or have laid down their lives in Latin America and other places for the sake of the gospel and for those for whom God has a preferential option — the poor, the orphan, the alien, the stranger?

The bishops, as our pastoral teachers, dogmatic and systematic theologians, and social and theological ethicists have been engaged in critical reflection on the issues of returning or resistant Catholics who look to the church for a reconciling embrace.[5] The teaching church and its members invoke the eucharistic grace of table fellowship as we together seek strength and support around these and other issues that require us to ponder well the meaning of the sacraments of community, forgiveness and communion.[6]

Reconciliation with as well as by the poor, the alienated, the frustrated and those who are furious within our familial contexts as well as beyond the reach of our own frameworks causes us to pause, perhaps, and to begin with one of the earliest rites of repentance which remains permanently etched within our eucharistic penitential rite. *Kyrie eleison, Christe eleison* — Lord, have mercy, Christ, have mercy. Or, in the words of the African American folk tune we know so well, we can say in truth, "It's me, it's me, it's me, O Lord, standing in the need of prayer." And we know the comfort and the empowerment of our enduring ecclesial response: "May Almighty God have mercy on *us,* forgive *us our* sins, and bring *us* to everlasting life."

In the Eucharistic Prayers for Masses of Reconciliation, which were prepared for the 1975 Holy Year and are now included in the sacramentary, the church through its ministers prays:

> God of love and mercy, you are always ready to forgive; we are sinners, and you invite us to trust in your mercy. Time and time again we broke your covenant, but you did not abandon us. Instead, through your Son, Jesus Christ our Lord, you bound yourself ever more closely to the human family by a bond that never can be broken.[7]

Pope John Paul II, in his post-synodal apostolic exhortation *Reconciliatio et Paenitentia (Reconciliation and Penance),* expresses these same thoughts despite the fact that the document does not stress changing society and its sinful structures,[8] as his other documents have and as did the 1983 Synod:

> The history of salvation — the salvation of the whole world of humanity, as well as of every human being of whatever period — is the wonderful history of a reconciliation: the reconciliation whereby God, as Father, in the blood and cross of his Son made man, reconciles *the world* to himself and thus brings into being a new family of these who have been reconciled.[9]

This primordial, sacramental mystery of reconciliation lies at the very core of the church, for it was and still is the mission of Jesus. Every time we celebrate the eucharist we proclaim that his blood "is shed . . . for all so that sins may be forgiven." By sharing in the "one bread and one cup," we become one body, the church. James Dallen has said regarding the future of reconciliation in the church and world today,

> What is really at risk is what it means for us to be church today. The personal sense of sin and repentance is admittedly at risk, but more importantly, the character of ecclesial identity and mission is endangered

by our failure to appreciate the true nature of this sacrament as communal reconciliation rather than individual forgiveness. Confusion, in fact, goes beyond names to mirror a lack of clarity regarding what our communities of faith are to be *in a changing world* and to show a lack of resolution in following through on the commitments made at Vatican Council II.[10]

This article will explore the arguments that the nature of reconciliation in the pastoral context of today's church and world must take seriously the connections between our understandings of social and individual sin and reconciliation if there is to be a future for this fundamental element of what it means to be redeemed, that is, to be reconciled to God and to one another, both as individuals and as a community, in Christ.

My arguments are constructed on the ecclesial and liturgical foundations that none of us is initiated or admitted as an atomized agent (e.g., an unconnected, privatized, totally alienated and unrelated individual) to the sacraments that emphasize the forgiveness, healing and unity of the intimately related, connected, social and sanctified community of the faithful. There is always the presence and the provident relationship of the "others" as sponsors, confessors, presiders, spiritual directors, fellow disciples, penitents and cocommunicants to fill out the injunction of Jesus' promise of his healing, forgiving and sustaining presence: "Where two or three are gathered in my name, there am I in the midst of them."[11] I will argue later in a more focused way concerning the importance of this christocentric dynamic in the experience and expression of reconciliation.

My major theological and ethical argument in a symposium subtitled "Reconciliation and ReMembering Church" will be based on a womanist[12] ethical understanding of the place and importance of the call to personal and public anamnesis, and to an emancipatory form and praxis of reconciliation for the church in a communal or social context of a redeemed and redeeming world. Church is the basic sacrament described and discussed in this essay. Church community is the most striking presentation to humanity of the reconciliation accomplished by God in Christ.[13] Especially in the community of the faithful assembled to baptize and to do eucharist, I argue that the church presents itself as "the universal sacrament of salvation."[14]

Reconciliation for the Church in the Context of a Redeemed World

The second creation account in Genesis confronts the reality of sin and describes the sinful condition of the world.[15] From the beginning, people sinned, and sin brought evil and alienation into society. This sinful situation is social and collective, and it becomes intensified through personal sin.[16] But God promised to deliver Adam and Eve and their descendants from this alienating condition. At times the Hebrew Scriptures describe YHWH's liberating efforts in terms of the kingdom of God or the kingdom of YHWH.[17] This kingdom, already present in the world, is moving toward final completion.

Jesus centered his life and teaching on the kingdom of God.[18] For our purposes, we can understand the kingdom as God's presence in a redeemed and redeeming world. The Hebrew and Christian scriptures describe this presence as freeing people as a community from brokenness and sin, and moving them toward health and wholeness. To better appreciate the kingdom as it applies to reconciliation, we will consider sin as alienation and look first at the relationship between the kingdom and reconciliation.

The Hebrew scriptures describe sin in a variety of ways: missing the mark, a twisted or distorted condition, alienation.[19] Each description implies that sin makes it difficult to become a whole person because it sets up a barrier to personal and community wholeness. The Israelite people had a very deep appreciation of the communal nature of sin. Sin always has a negative effect on the community or on subsequent generations; it is never a purely private matter. Even sin committed in one's heart leads to the development of patterns that eventually injure others. The Hebrew scriptures also were aware of the individual responsibility for sinful actions and the need for forgiveness.[20] These communal and individual dimensions are carried through in Jesus' teaching.

Jesus stresses the disorientation associated with sin. It blocks God within us, for when sin permeates a person's life, the choice is against God. Jesus continues the Hebrew tradition by stressing the communal and individual implications of sin. In speaking to individual sinners, he points out the need for conversion or change of heart.[21] By affirming Jesus' power over sin, the early Christian community identified Jesus as the most perfect representation of God's kingdom.

In the gospels, the kingdom of God is closely allied with healing and reconciliation. Jesus, as the model of the healing, reconciling kingdom, associates himself with poor people and sinners. He condemns poverty and sin, but by taking his place with the poor and sinners, he shows how God's presence can overcome human alienation and bring peace and hope. Out of obedience Jesus embraces the cross, a symbol of sin, and God raises him from the dead in testimony to Jesus' mission.[22] The crucifixion symbolizes the collective alienation caused by sin; the resurrection points to wholeness made possible for all who trust in God's forgiveness. From the vantage point of the kingdom, sin is the action of a person or people who refuse to live in the kingdom of God, in a redeemed and redeeming world which is made possible by the dynamic presence of Christ in the church.

Kingdom is a more encompassing concept than *church*. The latter ministers to the kingdom, to the redeemed and redeeming world, and shares God's healing and reconciling powers and christocentric presence. These powers touch the whole person — thus "ReMembering Church" or regrouping, reconciling the community of God's Chosen People. Reconciliation brings *shalom*, peace. This expression implies putting the pieces back together. Biblical wholeness includes psychic, physical, spiritual and social health and inclusivity. Today, a renewed appreciation of biblical wholeness and movements toward holistic spirituality acknowledge this kind of oneness or unitiveness with body and soul, with person and community, with cultures and societies that experience alienation, fragmentation or disunity.

Today as we consider reconciliation in the pastoral context of the church and the world, reconciliation might have a future if reconciliation in the church will take into account the person as a whole, considering the significance of an individual in relationship while considering how God communicates healing and forgiveness, in particular through a christocentric presence and dynamic of emancipatory love. God alone forgives and heals in a person's innermost self, but this healing and "re-membering" is incarnated through transformative love, sympathy and compassion, and above all, by justice enacted in and by the Christian community as well as by the institutional forms and agencies of the church which we call and claim as Roman Catholic in our world.

Reconciliation in the Context of Emancipatory Anamnesis

As a social ethicist and a liberation theology scholar, I am committed to transformative research that topples oppressive paradigms of human development that hinder both personal faith and social spirituality. That is to say, I teach that those models of faith development and spirituality which are inconsistent with the reality and worldview of people as unique creations of God must be critiqued. Models and methodologies of faith and spirituality which seek to understand the personal and communal epistemologies of diverse peoples must be developed and nurtured. These methods must affirm the uniqueness of people and honor their personhood while fostering a diversity and cultural plurality which are valued as well as appropriate in the sacramental and social life of the church.

This transformative motivational research should be able to invite critique of existing approaches to Roman Catholic efforts and experiences of reconciliation that are not focused on emancipatory theology, sacramentology, liturgy or similar kinds of justice-oriented environments. The results of such a loving and faithful critique should generate new ethical, theological and liturgical approaches to a forgiving, healing and liberating ecclesial ecology, environment and embodiment by the church. An answer to whether or not there is a future for reconciliation in the pastoral context of today's church and world depends in large part on developing prophetic, transformative efforts to defuse socially sinful realities and on providing tender, compassionate, pastoral solutions aimed at both individual and privatized concerns and problems.

My major argument is based on a womanist ethical understanding of the place and importance of the call to personal and public *anamnesis* and to an emancipatory form and praxis of reconciliation in a communal or social context of a redeemed and redeeming world. I argue that the principle of emancipatory critique and transformative theology, ethics and liturgy that embodies the expression and the experience of real reconciliation is to be found in some large measure within the praxis of *anamnesis,* or the practice of "the great remembrance."

This is the portion of the eucharistic liturgy, so called by the early Greek Christians, wherein we are to recall the acts of redemption that renew us, reconcile us and put us in solidarity with all God's people in all times and everywhere. The call to *anamnesis,* to remember, is quintessential; it is said that if we forget the past, we are destined to repeat it. May we never forget if we expect a future for reconciliation as God's great gift to the church and the world.

What shall we remember? Should we even attempt to strive to remember the blessedness of the reign of God promised to those who are poor, to those who are merciful, to those who mourn and to those who hunger and thirst for righteousness? After more than 500 years, should we try to remember with the many tribal peoples indigenous to this continent who were victims of genocide with the advent of Europeans?

How and in what way are we reconciled and in harmony with native peoples who are more than survivors today as they publicly claim and proclaim their heritage, their culture and their formative religious traditions while seeking to assist us in learning the essence of spiritualities that reconcile us with our Mother Earth, our Father Sky? Even as we are taught, we still resist efforts at real and deep ecology and prefer pollution, conspicuous consumption, wanton waste and habits of nonrecycling. Let us restore the theology and rite of reconciliation as the practice of "re-membering" as we seek to heal our alienation and fragmentation, not only with the church and the world but also with our earth and our environment.

In 1993 we were invited as a nation to remember the 130th anniversary of the Emancipation Proclamation, which was then on display briefly at the National Archives in Washington D.C., where it had not been exhibited in public since 1979. I want to remember it now as an image by which I might launch into a very small cameo reproduction of what a transformative theology, ethic and liturgy of reconciliation might mean if we are to claim the past as well as shape the future of a renewed understanding of a liberating sacrament of Christian unity.

Shawn Copeland, a distinguished womanist Catholic theologian[23] at Marquette University, shared with me her memories of the pilgrimage she made to see this fragile and faded document. She related to me how the tears came readily to her eyes as she read and traced out the words so faint and yet so fiery for the future full of hope promised for all African Americans. The words "forever free" leapt off the page at her and wound themselves around her mind and heart, and she remembered and reclaimed with renewed vigor and faith the meaning of her vocation as a recognized teacher, scholar and pastoral leader of the church in its efforts at reconciliation and liberation.

My own work has been focused on a description of a womanist ethics of care and on advocacy and pastoral healing for African American families experiencing abuse. The books I have written, as they have gained shape and content, have been in some form a way of remembering what it means to be set forever free, forever empowered to bless God with all our embodied and empowered, reconciled and reconciling selves.[24]

My work is a review of some women and families standing in the midst of that great cloud of witnesses who have gone on before us and who will come after us with the legacy of how we, like Langston Hughes' poem of "Mother to Son," have lifted as we have climbed, said to ourselves and to our families and to those in solidarity with us, "Now honey, don't you set down on the steps 'cause you finds it's kinda hard. . . . I'se still climbin' now, and life for me ain't been no crystal stair." Surely the responsorial psalm of womanist ethics is, in this context, "Try to remember, and if you remember, then follow, follow, follow."

A Womanist Ethic of Care

In cameo form, I want to share with you some constituent elements of a womanist ethics of care and then challenge and invite applications toward cultivating renewed, reconciled and reconciling lives in community — what I am calling a sacramental "emancipation proclamation." Try to remember, and if you remember, then follow, follow, follow.

I want to cite a brief excerpt from Toni Morrison's Pulitzer Prize-winning novel *Beloved*, a morally enriching and imaginative story of an extended and abused African American family and shaman-sheroe, the womanist Baby Suggs. Then I will offer an even briefer commentary on how this pericope is illustrative and illuminative of the essence of emancipatory reconciliation in which we are invited to share, to savor and to remember in the time to come.

Morrison conjures up reconciliation in a ritual of communal participation and in the context of a community "at home" yet alienated from the fullness of true freedom and peace because of racism, sexism and other oppressive ideologies of dominance and subordination. Morrison's narrator speaks:

Accepting no title of honor before her name, but allowing a small
caress after it, [Baby Suggs] became an unchurched preacher, one who
visited pulpits and opened her great heart to those who could use it.
In winter and fall she carried it to AME's and Baptists, Holinesses and
Sanctifieds, the Church of the Redeemer and the Redeemed. Uncalled,

unrobed, unanointed, she let her great heart beat in their presence. When warm weather came, Baby Suggs, holy, followed by every black man, woman, and child who could make it through, took her great heart to the clearing — a wide-open space cut deep in the woods. . . . In the heat of every Saturday afternoon, she sat in the clearing while the people waited among the trees.

After situating herself on a huge flat-sided rock, Baby Suggs bowed her head and prayed silently. The company watched her from the trees. They knew she was ready when she put her stick down. Then she shouted, "Let the children come!" and they ran from the trees toward her. "Let your mothers hear you laugh," she told them, and the woods rang. The adults looked on and could not help smiling.

Then, "Let the grown men come," she shouted. They stepped out one by one from among the ringing trees. "Let your wives and your children see you dance," she told them, and ground life shuddered under their feet.

Finally she called the women to her. "Cry," she told them, "for the living and the dead. Just cry." And without covering their eyes, the women let loose.

It started that way: laughing children, dancing men, crying women, and then it got mixed up. Women stopped crying and danced; men sat down and cried; children danced, women laughed, men cried until, exhausted and riven, all and each lay about the clearing damp and gasping for breath. In the silence that followed, Baby Suggs, holy, offered up to them her great big heart.

She did not tell them to clean up their lives or to go and sin no more. She did not tell them they were the blessed of the earth, its inheriting meek, or its glory bound pure.

She told them that the only grace they could have was the grace they could imagine. That if they could not see it, they would not have it. . . . Saying no more, she stood up then and danced with her twisted hip the rest of what her heart had to say while the others opened their mouths and gave her the music. Long notes held until the four-part harmony was perfect enough for their deeply loved flesh.[25]

Without intruding upon or appropriating the intended meaning of this pericope, I want to indicate that I believe that what is described here has the descriptive and paradigmatic elements for providing a renewed understanding of the *Rite of Reconciliation* that has a future for the church and the world as James Lopresti describes in his essay *Penance: A Reform Proposal for the Rite.*

In this seminal essay, Lopresti invites consideration of what people in trouble do to relieve their troubles. Lopresti lists four points, postulating that we may find in this often unfocused redemptive search some hints at the way reconciliation may be making its appearance in spite of the church's institutional short-sightedness. In summary, Lopresti says:

1. People in trouble connect with others who suffer the same deprivation, malaise or captivity.
2. People in trouble seek out others who have navigated these same disturbed waters at least slightly ahead of them.
3. People in trouble find people of wisdom and special expertise who will meet their needs.
4. People in trouble learn that relief usually comes slowly and with effort, and often in well marked stages.

In some ways, each of these present-day components of relief from trouble could be a realization of the God-touched human spirit yearning for and reaching out toward the integrity and wholeness we are meant to have.[26]

Lopresti adroitly points out that to be in trouble is not necessarily to be in sin. This is salutary advice for those of us who are seeking to focus on issues of reconciliation with returning or alienated Catholics and seeking to provide credible strategies for ministers looking for support and help. Yet there seems to be an understanding of sin, or perhaps the effects of sin, implied in these examples of people in trouble. Here Lopresti reconnects the meaning of the church as the principal sacrament of unity and reconciliation in much the same way Toni Morrison relates the assembly of poor, "in trouble" disenfranchised African American people who are reconciled by their ritual of moving together in harmony with Baby Suggs and implicitly with the christological dynamic presence of "the Lord of the Dance."

In consonance with this rich literary image of Morrison's, Lopresti continues his own commentary of a proposal for a renewed *Rite of Penance:*

> The church is meant to be a sign in the world of Christ's victory over sin. It is not that the church is the place where there is never any stagnation and alienation, but that the behavior of the people who call themselves church is manifestly moving away from alienation. It is a behavior that *enfleshes* a commitment to seek out deep unity, peace and harmony, and to seek it out in witness to the world. In other words, the church behaves in such a way that others who see the church may themselves trust their yearnings for bonds forged at a deeper level and for a fuller completion. The church is a reconciling agent in the world inasmuch as it is a living witness to belief in the opposite of alienation and stagnation. It empowers people to take hold of the Spirit of God planted in us all and to believe in our blessed destiny.[27]

In the emotionally moving pericope from novelist Toni Morrison we are able to gain a glimpse of the context of reconciliation from alienation as it appears in the context of a faithful and believing community's life and worship. Lopresti claims that there are different kinds of alienation, each of which calls for specific approaches to reconciliation. I argue with necessarily brief reference to his theory that all three approaches to understanding alienation and to establishing the marks of reconciliation are found here within the picture provided by Morrison.[28]

I tentatively and selectively make the claim that the approaches to reconciliation are indeed resonant with a womanist ethic of care which specifically responds to reconciliation with an unmistakable and concomitant call to social as well as personal liberation. This call and response are available for reflection and for application by those who are actively working toward a reform of the rite of reconciliation if it is to have a future in the church and world. The goal of reconciliation, then, is not mere reactivated membership but active participation in the common life of the People of God. The process will be different for different people, claims Lopresti. Let us look at each form of alienation in its turn as he describes them. Within the context of the differences, the place of the rite of penance as a means of attaining reconciliation will emerge. I will offer womanist ethical considerations as an additional guide.

The three different kinds of alienation lifted up by Lopresti are: (1) alienation of the unawakened; (2) true alienation; and (3) and prophetic alienation.[29] This is by no means an exhaustive typology, but this threefold division will help achieve clarity about the varieties of human experience that must be understood as we address the matter of receiving people "back" into the church through a reformed rite of penance.

Alienation of the unawakened is the experience of those who have never heard the personal call to be an apostle or witness, who have yet to recognize that a place has been prepared for them at the table of the eucharist or at the table of human and Christian dignity and unconditionally positive regard. *True alienation* is a term for those who have heard the call of the gospel and at some point have rejected it. In the ancient church, true alienation was recognized in the complete rupture of common life. True alienation, then, is overcome not by forgiveness alone but by healing and liberation as well. Some absent themselves from the table for reasons that appear to be exactly the opposite from "true alienation" as described by Lopresti.

The prophetically alienated claim that those who do gather around the table are doing so inauthentically or invalidly or both. The issue is not whether their claim is warranted. To understand this form of alienation, we need only be able to discern their stance in relation to the community. The prophetically alienated take a stance over against the community because of what they claim to be the community's own failure or sin. In the past, doctrinal or juridical questions may have caused the separation. Today it is usually a matter of disagreement about moral principles. For example, it may be the teaching church's position on abortion and reproductive rights and responsibilities. It may be the believing church's often negative attitude about the acceptability of variant lifestyles, for example, the humanity, integrity, dignity and acceptability of gay and lesbian persons and their partners in relationship. It may be disputes over gender roles in leadership, for example, the rights and roles of women in liturgical, sacramental and pastoral jurisdiction and authority.

Lopresti predicates that for the *Rite of Penance* to have a future in the church and the world, there are four markers for closing the distance in each instance of the different kinds of alienation described. The markers are: (1) hearing the gospel announced; (2) responding to the gospel announcement; (3) acquiring a new set of relationships to God and world; and (4) celebrating the reconciled life.[30] From these markers, Lopresti develops what he considers a way to think about the rite of penance in light of the Christian initiation experience. I leave you to his work for thoughtful reflection, both in reviewing the responsive portion by Toni Morrison and in applying these markers to other cultural, social and individual case studies in reconciliation rituals and rites.

In brief, what I want you to remember about a womanist ethics of care in relation to reconciliation are the following premises, which are potentially adaptable to other strategies for future holistic pastoral forms of social and individual reconciliation in the church and world.

A womanist ethic of care fostering true reconciliation is one that is born in refusals to endure with grace the arrogance, indifference, hostility and damage of oppressively sexist, classist, racist environments. A womanist ethic of care is fueled by bonds among black women and other people of color as well as those of the dominant culture who care, forged in experiments to create better environments now and in the future and tried by commitments to overcome damage already done. Womanist ethics benefits from experience, choices we have already faced. Womanist ethics invites reflection upon character and social relationships developed under socio-political norms, reflection upon possibilities of bringing about transformative change (*metanoia* in its deepest sense) and of making a difference through reconciliation linked to liberation.[31]

Womanist ethics interests me especially in relation to problems of moral agency and activism under oppression when there is obvious need for repentance and reconciliation. If oppressive institutions stifle and stunt the moral development of the oppressed and disenfranchised, how is it possible, or what does it mean, "to announce good news to the poor, to set at liberty them that are held captive, to announce a year of favor from our God"?[32] Can you remember what there is in your vocation or calling to express, to experience, and to practice reconciliation as it relates to being "forever free"? Anamnesis is necessary to obtaining a future for real reconciliation in the church and in the world.

Can you remember what it is to resist social evil as well as individualized oppression wherever it exists in your understanding and experience of globalization and of a church that styles itself as "universal" in its outreach and in its "welcome home"? Because of transformative teaching, preaching and ministering that serve as emancipatory efforts at reconciliation, will you remember that it is always necessary to make morally responsible choices, to become better and stronger moral agents? that it is always necessary to develop character and endurance that doesn't wimp out?

Returning to our image of the Emancipation Proclamation document, can we imagine what this kind of civil religion announcement meant to a people silenced and without a voice in so many ways? It is no accident that our own Negro National Anthem is titled "Lift Every Voice and Sing." The slave narratives recount that "ol' white preachers used to talk wid dey tongues widdout sayin' nothin; but Jesus told us slaves to talk wid our hearts." These words of an ex-slave suggest that ideas cannot be divorced from the individuals who create and share them.

The theme of talking with the heart taps the womanist ethic of caring, an alternative epistemology most often used intuitively by black women. Just as the ex-slave used the wisdom of her heart to reject the ideas of the preachers who talked "wid dey tongues widdout sayin' nothin'," we must pray with our acts, our great hearts which are not ashamed to show the totality of our love in our praxis.

A transformative praxis connected to the sacraments that reflect emancipatory reconciliation suggests that as one imbibes and embodies a personal emancipation proclamation and acts out a public or social ethic of liberation, our gifts of expressiveness, emotions, and empathy, one becomes more like that unnamed woman of the gospel who anointed Jesus and ministered to his body lavishly. And for her service he remembered and reconciled her as "forever free" in our proclamation of Good News. This evangelical story is emblematic of a never-to-be-forgotten expression and rite of reconciliation performed for our benefit and imitation by Jesus the Lord.

A Future for Reconciliatory Emancipation

The problem of relating the reconciling and unitive meanings of the Christian gospel, church teachings and the sacraments with their socially emancipative and liberative meanings has been an ongoing concern wherever traditional North Atlantic theologies and ethics have come into conversation, and often conflict, with more recent liberation theologies. For example, the conversation became conflictual concerning the South African *Kairos Document*,[33] which argues that primacy given to reconciliation meanings of the gospel, and especially to church teaching, is often, especially in South Africa, a way to mask injustice and oppression. The document powerfully argues that justice and liberation must occur as a condition for authentic ecumenical reconciliation among and in the Christian churches.

At this concluding point, however, I am more concerned with making the simpler closing argument that both reconciliatory and emancipative elements belong together in any pastoral understanding of the meaning of Roman Catholic teaching and practice of reconciliation. Hence, the final feature to note about "reconciliatory emancipation" — the name I have assigned to preparing a future in which reconciliation in the pastoral context of the church and world might actually exist — is that it must fuse both reconciliatory and emancipative dimensions.[34]

Both reconciliation and liberation/emancipation are inextricably joined components of the discursive elements of the Roman Catholic tradition (scriptures, creeds, doctrines). They are at least implicitly inseparable in our tradition's extradiscursive elements (rituals, ministries, communal dynamics, institutional structure). More importantly, explicit reference to the special character of the christocentric dynamic made real in reconciliation as both reconciliatory and emancipative enables us to directly address the two most important prongs of postmodern alienating dilemmas. These twin and deadly dilemmas which keep us from completely claiming reconciliation in its diverse but interrelated religious and ritual expressions and forms are: difference[35] (affirming plurality) and domination[36] (resisting oppression).

In my proposed renaming or reclaiming, then, of the pastoral term "reconciliatory emancipation," the reconciliatory element must be stressed, making possible a christocentric presence addressed to the contemporary realities of difference and lack of unity resident amidst the intense and recalcitrant pluralism in our church and world. The emancipatory element must be equally stressed to empower resistance to an ubiquitous and universal experience of unjust dominance and systemic exploitation. Alienating responses to human difference and deliberate unjust domination are defeated in the reclamation and fusing of the name and claim for a kind of "reconciliatory emancipation." The two elements expressed in the term "reconciliatory emancipation" work together to structure the salvific communal dynamic of sacramental realities toward an end of alienating and destructive responses to human difference and of oppressive forms of domination.

In summary, what I have argued in broad, general terms but with paradigmatic exemplification by means of womanist experience and ethical reflection is that the reconciliation we are reviewing must not simply address individual alienation and religious dislocation but it must redress social, racial and economic differences by seeking a valuation of these experiences that leads to social, sacramental expressions of communities of sacred solidarity and of covenantal alliances of grace and mercy.

The reconciliatory emancipation for which I am arguing must not just proclaim individual, privatized forgiveness and deliverance but must do so through a redress of specific social and public expressions of oppression and repression in our era of church and world history, from which profound and prolific deliverance is needed. Racism, sexism, homophobia and militarism are merely large-scale indices of individual expressions of sin for which we seek absolution, reconciliation and renewed relations of harmony and justice, and for which we must renew our practices of repentance and of restored structures of solidarity which sustain and support a discipleship of equals and a kingdom of peace.

In considering whether "there is a future for reconciliation in the pastoral context of today's church and world," my answer is one hedged on the bet of emerging performative expressions of repentance. My hope is based on renewed liberational understandings which effectively challenge the devastating and devaluing relationships of social and individual sin and the alienation of persons, constituencies and communities. My faith is focused on what I take to be an abiding desire in and through our church for active and enthusiastic engagement in emancipatory forms of personal and public commitment to sacramental processes of renewal in the midst of all the People of God.

For Pastoral Reflection and Response

It may seem strange or surprising to begin a discussion of sacramental reconciliation from the viewpoint of social ethics. However, it is most appropriate for three reasons. First, the theology of the 1973 *Rite of Penance* emphasizes the social and ecclesial nature of the sacrament (see, for example, paragraphs 3–5 and the rites of reconciliation of several penitents). Second, the broader foundation for the sacrament is the mystery of Christ's reconciliation of the world to God. This once-and-for-all act continually reminds and challenges us that the ministry and celebration of reconciliation is not just for the salvation of individuals but for the life of the world. Third, "the meaning of the sacraments of community, forgiveness and communion" contain in them a compelling vision of how we are to live in our world, how we are to understand and structure it. In other words, our liturgical celebrations — reconciliation no less than baptism and eucharist — present and engage us in the thick of God's reign.

This is the genius of Dr. Eugene's presentation. She places the question of the future of reconciliation in the liturgical context of *anamnesis,* the great remembrance of "the acts of redemption that renew us, reconcile us, and put us in solidarity with all of God's people in all times and everywhere." She grapples with an answer as she raises, from a womanist perspective, an ethics of care. This care is no superficial good will but the prophetic process of understanding profoundly the powerlessness and destruction sin and evil create, and of crying out compassionately and insistently until God and humankind are awakened to forgiveness, healing and emancipation. Care is a process of remembering that tells "the narrative of the lie" and "the narrative of the truth" — as Robert Schreiter calls them,[1] the stories of wretched and scandalous sin and evil, and the stories of saving grace.

A first pastoral concern is how we remember the stories of the social sins of our time: racism, militarism, sexism, homophobia, consumerism, classism, ageism, the rape of the earth's resources, and so on. How are these sins and evils manifest in the immediate lives of our parishioners? Where are they present in our neighborhoods, workplaces, cities and towns, church — and our own hearts? Preaching, lifelong religious formation and the church's and the parish's witness in the community and the world combine to bring us to an ever deeper understanding of the ruptures of human and ecclesial communion, and of the wholeness and truth to which we are invited. The kind of social analysis we do as a parish, diocese and church will be crucial here. Have we listened deeply and in all directions? Have we refrained from taking sides except to discern where the

Holy Spirit is at work? Are we acting on options that are compatible with the gospel message?

It is important also to remember that remembering takes time, often incredible amounts of it. Reconciliation does not happen simply by willing it or scheduling it; the making of peace in the Middle East or the finding of economic justice in Latin America are abundant proof of that. Reconciliation occurs in "God's good time," that intersection of God's many-faceted grace, the free cooperation of individuals, the church's action and the particular circumstances of time and place.[2] Pastorally, the challenge is to keep the energy and resources of the church fully active for reconciliation while waiting patiently for the Spirit of the Risen One to bring it to fulfillment, allowing individual people and groups the time to tell their stories fully. It will take time to develop "models and methodologies of faith and spirituality" that understand the expression of diverse peoples and affirm and honor the plurality of the church and world. It will take time to create better environments that will overcome and transform the damage done by sin and evil.

Time, however, is not the only thing it will take to discern God's work of reconciliation; it will take imagination as well. In a society rife with litigation but little justice, and in a world rife with greed and violence, we have a poverty of imagination around "reconciliatory emancipation." This dearth is due in large part to the fact that our symbol system — the liturgical texts and rituals of reconciliation — are so sparse. We need robust symbols of reconciliation to feed our imaginations for strategies of reconciliation. But robust symbols arise from depth experiences, and so we are caught in a vicious cycle.

A pastoral task still ahead of us is to surface texts and rituals that have an "anamnetic" power. We need prayers, songs, proclamations and gestures that help us remember the power of evil in our world and the greater and transforming power of God's grace. The two eucharistic prayers of reconciliation and the scrutinies are splendid examples of such anamnesis. However, our rites of penance, the reproaches on Good Friday, the penitential practice appropriate to our time, our observance of Lent, our preaching the Just Word and our witness as church at the local level remain anemic instruments for expressing and deepening reconciliation in Christ. The church's ministers need to join with poets, novelists, sculptors, painters, dancers, dramatists and any who use their imaginations to find the symbols of scripture and life that help us remember lies and truth so that we can be "forever free."

This response was provided by Robert J. Kennedy.

Alienation in the Catholic Church Today
Evidence from the Catholic Pluralism Project

James D. Davidson

My purposes here are to report data from the Catholic Pluralism Project showing the extent of alienation in the church today and to explain why some Catholics are more alienated than others. I will first introduce the Catholic Pluralism Project and then summarize what I mean by the term "alienation." Next, I will describe the overall extent of alienation among the Catholics who participated in the project and use a sociological framework to explain variations in the degree of alienation among Catholics. Finally, I will suggest some implications these findings have for clergy and lay leaders interested in reconciliation.

Catholic Pluralism Project

The goals of the Catholic Pluralism Project are to describe and explain variations in faith and morals.[1] With regard to faith, we are examining three types of religious practices: pre–Vatican II practices, such as saying the rosary and going to private confession; post–Vatican II practices, such as reading the Bible and attending prayer groups; and pan–Vatican II practices, such as attending Mass and receiving Holy Communion. We also are distinguishing among three types of belief: pre–Vatican II emphases on issues such as obedience and the Catholic Church as the "one true Church"; post–Vatican II beliefs about matters such as the personal nature of faith and the importance of the laity; and pan–Vatican II beliefs such as Incarnation and Resurrection. We are examining two dimensions of morality: sexual morality (e.g., birth control, abortion, etc.) and social teachings (e.g., the church's role in social issues, the morality of economic decisions that increase poverty, etc.).

We are using sociological theory to show how the personal attributes Catholics are born with affect the way they are raised and the experiences they have over the course of their adult lives. But, our theory says that we are more than products of our environments. We also assess our upbringing and our life experiences, arriving at some sense of who we are (our self-concepts) and what the costs and benefits of being Catholic are (our self-interests). It is on the basis of these self-concepts and self-interests that Catholics decide what to believe and how to practice their faith (see figure 1).

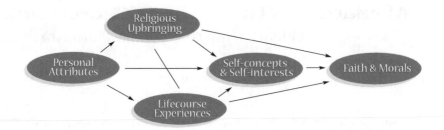

We are testing these ideas using an inductive method, which is producing several kinds of data. We have done lengthy interviews with selected Catholics of all ages. We also have done focus groups with three generations of Catholics: people who were born and raised prior to Vatican II; people who experienced both the "old church" in the 1950s and Vatican Council II (1962–1965) during their formative years; and, finally, young Catholics who have been raised entirely in the post–Vatican II church. We also have done a statewide survey of more than 4,000 Catholics in all five of Indiana's dioceses. We had an exceptionally high return rate (57 percent) on a very lengthy instrument that included questions on all aspects of our theory.[2] We are now doing a national telephone poll. Those results will be available by fall 1995.[3]

We have reported our results in meetings with Indiana's five bishops and their staffs. We also issued a series of news releases which have appeared in secular and diocesan newspapers throughout the state of Indiana. We are now engaged in a series of meetings with directors of religious education. The response has been very gratifying. Church leaders throughout the state are examining our results to see how they might reach out to different types of Catholics in new and more effective ways.

Alienation

I think of alienation in terms of Catholics' self-concepts. Some people identify with the church a great deal; others do not. Some people claim the church as their own; others don't feel they fit in. Some cannot imagine being anything but Catholic; others can imagine belonging to some other faith group. Some people feel as if they are part of the church; others feel apart from it. Some internalize church norms and values; others do not. Some people feel they are religious; others do not. Alienation exists to the extent that Catholics do not identify with the church, do not feel they are part of the church, can imagine themselves as members of another faith group, do not feel they fit into the church, feel apart from the church, and do not internalize church norms and values.

I also think of alienation in terms of Catholics' self-interests. Some think they have benefited enormously from being Catholic; others feel they've paid a big price for being Catholic. Some feel it has been advantageous to be Catholic;

others say it has been disadvantageous. Some feel they've got a lot to gain from staying involved; others don't. Alienation prevails to the extent that Catholics say that the costs of being in the church outweigh the benefits.

These two dimensions of alienation overlap to a great extent. People who are least inclined to identify with the church also are least likely to feel they have benefited from being Catholic. People who don't think there is any benefit to being Catholic tend not to identify with the church. Self-concepts and self-interests certainly are not identical, but they tend to go hand in hand. Therefore, Catholics who identify with the church and feel they have benefited from being part of the church are not alienated. People who do not identify with the church and do not see any benefit from being Catholic are.[4]

Extent of Alienation

Given these definitions, how alienated are Catholics today? To what extent do Catholics no longer identify with the church? To what extent do they not see any advantage to being Catholic? The answer partly depends on whether you include "fallen away" Catholics with people who are still in the church.

"Fallen away" Catholics are not involved in the church but also have not converted to any other religion. According to canon law, even though these people are not parish members, they are still Catholic.

Dean Hoge's book *Converts, Dropouts, Returnees*[5] shows that fallen away Catholics are highly alienated from the church. Most dropouts no longer have strong Catholic identities, though some do. Most also say they no longer have any reason to be Catholic. In fact, many feel that their lives have improved since they left the church. As a result, they do not attend church very often, and religious belief is not a very important part of their lives.

When we examine people who remain in the church (i.e., people who are on parish rolls), we find much less alienation. Here is a sample of how Indiana Catholics responded to several questions about their religious self-concepts.

97 percent said they need God's help to live good and decent lives.

78 percent said they cannot imagine being anything other than Catholic.

77 percent said their parishes are important parts of their lives.

67 percent believe that the Catholic Church is the one true church.

41 percent said they are quite or very religious; 44 percent said they are fairly religious.

These data suggest that, among people in parishes, Catholic identity is quite strong. Most Catholics still think there is something special about being Catholic, though some are not so sure. Most think of themselves as pretty religious, though some do not. Most cannot imagine being anything but Catholic; some can.

What did Catholics say about the costs and benefits of being in the church?

94 percent said that being Catholic has given them a solid moral foundation.

89 percent said their parishes help them know God's love and care for them.

When asked to grade the pope's leadership from A to F, 78 percent gave him As and Bs.

76 percent said the homilies at their parishes are very well done.

75 percent denied having any emotional scars from being brought up Catholic.

When asked to grade their parishes in terms of meeting their spiritual needs, 70 percent gave them As and Bs.

50 percent said they have never been discriminated against because they are Catholic; 30 percent said they have felt discrimination once or twice; 18 percent said several times; only 2 percent said frequently.

Once again, most Catholics seem to feel that the benefits of being Catholic outweigh the costs. Most feel that being Catholic has helped them; some are not so sure. Most think there is something to be gained by staying in the church, though some disagree.

These results suggest overall that Catholic parishioners are not as alienated as we sometimes think they are, and they certainly are not as alienated as Catholics who are no longer active. These data are consistent with other recent polls.[6] We expect to find a similar pattern when we analyze the data from the last stage of the Catholic Pluralism Project, our national telephone poll.

Which Catholics Are Most and Least Alienated?

Nonetheless, some parishioners are more alienated than others. Being Catholic and being religious are not very important issues for some parishioners, and some feel that being Catholic is more of a burden than a benefit. Who are these people?

Starting with the personal attributes cell in our model (see figure 1), we sorted Indiana Catholics according to the following variables: age cohort (pre–Vatican II, born before 1941; Vatican II, born 1941–1960; post–Vatican II, born 1961–1976); race and ethnicity (black, white, Latino); gender (male and female); generation in the United States (first, second, and third or more); educational level (high to low); and family income (high to low).

Four variables were consistently and highly related to alienation: age cohort, generation in the United States, education and income. Young, third-generation, highly educated and high-income Catholics tended to be most alienated. These groups were least likely to identify with the church, least inclined to think of themselves as religious, least likely to report that they had benefited from being Catholic, least satisfied with their parishes and most likely to disagree with official church teachings.

The least alienated Catholics tended to be older, first-generation Americans with limited educations and relatively low incomes. Members of these groups were most likely to say they could not imagine being anything but Catholic, most likely to say religion is an important part of their lives, most likely to say they had benefited from being Catholic, most satisfied with their parishes and most likely to agree with Vatican policies on issues such as ordination.

Women were more likely to identify with the church than men and were somewhat more likely to say they have benefited from being Catholic. However, gender did not have much effect on Catholics' satisfaction with their parishes or their satisfaction with Vatican policies.

The effects of race and ethnicity were quite mixed and not as large. Latinos were most likely to identify with the church, followed by whites, then blacks. Blacks and Latinos were more inclined to say they had benefited from being Catholic than whites. Overall, the results suggest that blacks were most alienated, Latinos least. Whites fell in between.

Explaining Alienation

Why are some Catholics more alienated than others? Our theoretical model suggests that the different attributes people are born with set their lives in motion. These attributes affect the way people are raised and their lifecourse experiences. Learning theory[7] tells us that in childhood and during their adult years, people learn by interacting with the people around them and the people they admire most. They learn by imitating parents, peers, spouses, priests and sisters, and coworkers. These "significant others" also use rewards to encourage certain types of behavior and punishments to discourage others. These childhood and lifecourse experiences affect people's religious self-concepts and self-interests. They foster strong Catholic identities and important benefits among some Catholics; they lead to alienation among some others.

Let me illustrate how this theory works by focusing on the pre–Vatican II, Vatican II, and post–Vatican II age cohorts because, of all the personal attributes we have examined, these consistently have had the largest effects on Catholics' beliefs and practices. These three generations were raised in very different ways.

Older Catholics were taught by priests and nuns. They learned their faith by memorizing the questions and answers in the Baltimore Catechism. They learned that the Catholic Church is "the one true church." They learned that the church is an end in itself, something they should support no matter what. They learned that the church is important in all facets of one's life, from "womb to tomb." They developed a vivid Catholic language consisting of words such as "original sin," "veneration of the cross," "novenas," "mortal sin," "rosary beads," "Vicar of Christ," "venial sin," "Blessed Virgin Mary," and "Mystical Body of Christ." They learned the importance of the sacraments and of relying on the church for help at all the crucial times of their lives. They learned to obey priests and nuns, and to fear hell. These pre–Vatican II experiences fostered high levels of Catholic identity and a sense that there were enormous benefits from being Catholic.

Catholics who experienced their formative years during the 1950s and 1960s had many of these same experiences during their early years, but the church changed dramatically during their high school and college years. In a sense, they were born with one foot in the old church (pre–Vatican II) and one in the new (post–Vatican II). They were part of the shift from Latin to English; from Gregorian chant to folk music; from organs to guitars; from an emphasis on sexual purity to an emphasis on peace and justice; from natural-law ethics to consequentialism (an emphasis on the context and consequences of behavior); from faith as obligation to faith as personal choice; from other-worldliness to this-worldliness; from particularism (i.e., the superiority of Catholicism) to ecumenism (i.e., an emphasis on how much Catholicism has in common with Protestant denominations). The dramatic changes this generation of Catholics experienced shook some people's Catholic identity and their confidence about the benefits of staying in the church.

Post–Vatican II Catholics have been raised very differently. Most of their religion teachers have been lay people. They have been taught that they are Christians first, Catholics second. They are more likely to talk about being Christian than they are to think of themselves as Catholics. When you listen to them talk, they speak a sort of generic Christian language; they do not have much of a specifically Catholic language at all. They also have learned a very personal approach to faith. They have been taught that they are on their own faith journeys and that it is up to them to choose their faith; whether that means being Catholic or something else is up to them. They have been taught a more instrumental view of the church: Participate in the church as long as it serves your needs; when and if it doesn't, explore other options. As a result, young Catholics do not have especially strong Catholic identities and are not as sure about the benefits of being in the church.

Given these different religious upbringings, it is no wonder that pre–Vatican II Catholics feel most integrated into the church and post–Vatican II Catholics are most alienated. For example, 78 percent of pre–Vatican II Catholics said that they cannot imagine being anything other than Catholic, and 55 percent scored high on our index of costs and benefits. Fifty-five percent of Vatican II Catholics have strong Catholic identities, and 36 percent scored high on our self-interest index. Only 48 percent of post–Vatican II Catholics are unconditionally aligned with the church, and only 34 percent said they have benefited highly from being Catholic.

Lifecourse experiences also affect alienation. One lifecourse factor is the extent to which Catholics have "experiences of the holy." Two-thirds of Indiana Catholics said that God takes care of them when they need help; 59 percent feel that God loves them; 56 percent said that God answers their prayers. The fact that a majority of Catholics have such experiences contributes to the relatively high levels of Catholic identity and to parishioners' reports that the benefits of being Catholic outweigh the costs. Moreover, there was a strong negative correlation between these holiness experiences and alienation. People who had not had these experiences as often were much more alienated, both in terms of self-concept and self-interest.

Implications

What do these results imply for clergy and lay leaders interested in reconciliation? They have at least three implications.

First, they suggest that there is far more alienation among fallen-away Catholics than there is among people who are still in the church. Working with fallen-away Catholics is likely to be much more difficult, because most of them have established lifestyles which now reinforce their alienation from the church (such as marrying non-Catholics and investing in other activities which they find more rewarding than being active in the church). Working with alienated people who are still in the church also is difficult but may be more productive, since the obstacles to be overcome may not be quite as severe.

Second, alienation levels seem to be highest among the most resourceful people in the church (e.g., the youngest, most assimilated, most educated and most affluent). As the older age cohort is replaced by middle-aged and younger Catholics, levels of alienation are likely to increase in the years ahead. Left untreated, this situation will rob the church of many important human and economic resources in the years ahead. Thus, it is in the church's interest to promote Catholic identity and demonstrate the benefits of being in the church.

Third, alienation is the result of the way some people are raised and their lifecourse experiences, both inside and outside the church. If we want to reduce alienation, we need to alter childhood experiences that diminish some people's identification with the church and their appreciation of the benefits of being Catholic. For example, without diminishing efforts to appreciate our common heritage with other Christian faiths, religious educators might need to reassert the idea that there also is something special about being Catholic. That can be done by emphasizing at least two issues which seem important to all Catholics, regardless of their other differences: the church's history as the oldest Christian faith and the mystery of the eucharist, where bread and wine are transformed into the Body and Blood of Christ.

We also need to address lifecourse experiences that foster Catholic identity and foster awareness of the ways one can benefit from being involved in the church. Experiences of the holy could be one focal point for such efforts. The more church leaders forge close connections between the sacraments and experiences of the holy, the more Catholics can appreciate their Catholic heritage and the spiritual benefits of belonging to the church. We also need to demonstrate how the church can help members deal with worldly needs such as raising children, coping with problems at work and dealing with death in one's family.

Taking steps in these directions will help to stifle predictable trends toward increased alienation. Failure to act will ensure more alienation among the people of God in the years ahead.

For Pastoral Reflection and Response

Those of us who have been or are involved in pastoral ministry rely on the research of sociologists (and experts and scholars in other fields) to help us define, evaluate and refine our thinking and methods with the people among whom we minister. Pastoral ministers know the stories and details of these people's lives; sociologists, taking a broader view, name characteristics and trends among them. Thus there is set up a creative dialogue that can provide insights for more effective ministry.

As we read this preliminary report on the Catholic Pluralism Project, we may feel affirmed by the data, or we may feel critiqued. We may be surprised at some of the specific pieces (e.g., the high level of satisfaction with homilies, or among women), or we may nod our heads in knowing agreement (e.g., the general lack of strong Catholic identity among the young). We may be comforted that Catholic parishioners are not as alienated as they are sometimes thought to be; we may be challenged by the difficulty of reaching out to and working with "fallen away" Catholics. And when we begin to put faces from our own ministries on these facts and figures, there is a blossoming of questions, insights and possibilities in the work of reconciliation. Here are several, offered simply to prime the pump of pastoral reflection and planning.

First, isn't it clear that the church (and the parish, as its most immediate manifestation) plays a powerful role in giving (or not giving) a sense of place and identity to people? The church/parish can be the place where people belong, where people feel grounded, where faith is nourished, interpreted and deepened. But because of that, it most often holds the possibility of producing alienation. Yet again, it also possesses the full resources of reconciliation. This powerful yet fluid position of the church and parish in people's lives and faith is an awesome, dangerous and joyful responsibility all at once.

We might say that one crucial finding of this project is that Catholics are made, not born. No matter what our age, we have been shaped by the way we were raised and the experiences we have had. So what does it mean to be Catholic? How are Catholics made?

This will lead us first to reflect on the adequacy of the parish programs and processes we offer to shape faith. How will these provide good memories of church and of God for people of all ages and situations? "Self-concept" and "self-interest" in relation to God and the church are served (or disabled) by sacramental preparation, youth ministry, religious education, liturgical celebration, preaching, the varieties of pastoral care and service, and witness in the wider community. We need to uncover in ever new ways the richness of Catholic sacrament, spirituality, morality, justice, devotion and mission. Anyone involved in the ministries of evangelization, initiation and reconciliation knows that the Catholic church has a rich store of treasures to offer our world and individual hearts. How will people know it is there and discover its depth?

We can approach the "Catholic identity" issue from another angle. If our self-concepts and self-interests determine our beliefs and practice, there is what we might call a spiritual direction question. What does God have to do with my life? How do I discern what is holy? These are vital questions for ministers in conversation with those who stay in the church and those who do not. It is heartening to know that most respondents said that their parishes helped them to know God's love and care for them. Yet the question remains, how does the church mediate "the Holy" for people? And how can the church touch those who hunger for "the Holy" but may not look to the church as an avenue? What communal and individual forms of spiritual direction are we now engaged in, or are possible, to help people know more deeply God's presence and promise in their lives?

Most centrally, of course, being Catholic means living a eucharistic life: all brothers and sisters, called together and shaped by the Word of God, giving thanks and praise, and, in communion with Christ and one another, going forth to love and serve the Lord. How will we unpack the mystery of living a eucharistic life so that people will enter it joyfully?

Reconciling is part of this eucharistic lifestyle and Catholic identity. Our experience of God brings a responsibility to deal with sin and brokenness. In the church sinners find a welcome and wisdom that leads to a breakthrough to new life in Christ. The call to holiness will not allow the church to ignore the alienated Catholic. To do so is to forget who we are as church. The challenge is for the church to communicate to alienated Catholics the great need the church has to be reconciled with them.

If we are going to engage in ministry with alienated Catholics, we have to ask who it is we are dealing with. This report from the Catholic Pluralism Project distinguishes between participating, alienated Catholics and those who are "fallen away" (or inactive, estranged). Or better, it helps us to name the factors that may lead to alienation, estrangement and inactivity: age, level of education and wealth, generation in the United States. Every person grapples with the deeper questions about the meaning of life, God, identity and a host of other core-touching issues. Every person has a unique story and so does not fit neatly into a category. People become alienated when their stories or answers no longer seem to fit and they cannot find the hearing or wisdom they need.

As we put names and faces to these "age cohorts" and try to minister with them, we need to ask: What are the distinctive needs of each group? What are the issues of hurt, alienation and reconciliation that we see in each, and more importantly, that each tells us about when we listen? They may be hurt, broken or estranged because of their current situation in life, because of church teachings or practices, or because of the actions or style of the ministers of the church themselves. Sometimes a "church event" (e.g., "Father didn't visit my mother when she was sick," or "I liked the Mass the way it used to be") becomes the alienated focal point for all the small hurts that have gathered and pooled unattended in someone's life.

In any and all circumstances of alienation — practicing or "fallen away," pre–Vatican II, Vatican II or post–Vatican II Catholics — the church's ministers will have to listen carefully and deeply to what people have to tell us. Each group will likely have its own language for expressing its needs, hurts, brokenness and hopes; and within each group, every person will have a unique story. When we meet alienated Catholics at baptisms and weddings, in times of illness and death, in sacramental programs and community projects, the church's ministers will be in that powerful but vulnerable spot where both alienation and reconciliation are possibilities. We need to be ready to listen and to wait, and to wait some more, for "the story beneath the story" to be told.

In a related way, it is important for pastoral ministers to remember that they too belong to one of these "age cohorts" and may themselves be alienated in some way by life's experiences, the church or the people they serve. Alienation and reconciliation is a two-way street, and ministers need to know and attend to themselves in order to be reconciling ministers.

Further, the church cannot be afraid to address the conditions that prevent it from serving the interests of its members. That is, we need to deal with the tensions created by the real lives of people, ministry with a compassionate heart and fidelity to tradition. Perhaps the most obvious issue here concerns the pastoral situations of separation, divorce and remarriage held in tension with the church's teachings and values about marriage and family life. How do we avoid collisions at the intersection of personal conscience, pastoral care, theological understandings and canon law? How do we handle those collisions when they occur? And more positively, how do we provide the fullness of life that the church offers for any person or group of persons who are caught in the dilemma of personal experience and conscience and the church's teaching and practice?

There is one more question (for now) about identity and about ministry that we must ask: Why would the church want alienated Catholics back? We may laugh at first at the question, but in relationship (and this is what alienation and reconciliation are really about), knowing why we miss someone's company gives us more of a reason to reconnect. We need to name those reasons clearly and honestly, and to understand the assumptions underlying them. Does the burden fall upon their shoulders only? Is our attitude "let them come to us"? What is the church willing to risk to re-establish relationships with our brothers and sisters?

The oral responses given at the symposium by Tom Ranzino, pastor of Saint George Church, Baton Rouge, Louisiana, and Therese Ann Kiefer, ASC, director of ongoing formation for the Congregation of Adorers of the Blood of Christ, Red Bud, Illinois, contributed greatly to these pastoral notes.

The Wounded Soul
Through the Lens of Pastoral Psychology

Paul J. Philibert, OP

The twentieth century is the age of psychology. Freud's *On the Interpretation of Dreams* was published in 1900 with dramatic flourish as a way of proposing psychoanalysis as the theory that would transform culture and history in this century. To a degree that Freud could hardly have imagined, his product — a theory of a soul divided between conscious and unconscious seeking wholeness through therapy — has become a dominant cultural influence of this century. Key ideas from psychiatry and clinical psychology have become part of the common store of explanations about life that most people grow up with.

Psychology explains that every child begins to learn about reality by becoming attached to the constellations of meaning and purpose offered by parents, especially by the mother. Every child receives existence as a gift and enters into the promise of a meaningful life through a long process of becoming. In the earliest years of life, the child's need for nurture and direction is so extreme that the child accedes to the wishes of authorities without resistance. At age two, however, children adopt the defense of saying "no," though they continue ultimately to maintain an overall compliance with adults. At age three, they often become precise in wanting things to be orderly. A factor of increasing importance is the cooperation — even conspiracy — of children four to seven in creating worlds of their own in momentary parentheses apart from parents, where in play and work together they first explore the originality of their own personalities.

Only after some 12 or 13 years of life do children begin to shake themselves loose from the authority of their parents and claim some sense of self-generated identity. There is an ironic twist about this much-celebrated adolescent rebellion: In the process of trying to become independent, young people tend to express themselves as counter-dependent (that is, doing just the opposite of what authorities seem to want of them), thereby failing to escape from a destiny determined for them by the wishes of others.[1] Before any consistent agenda of personal interests can develop, the adolescent must shake loose from the constraints of an over-developed dependency upon parents and teachers. Sometimes this transition is serene; often it is turbulent. Either way, there are usually misunderstandings, hurt feelings and some anger on both sides before this adolescent transition is completed.

Issues of sin, guilt and psychic brokenness are enmeshed in the dynamics of psychological development. To try to deal with the phenomena of fault and sin without placing them in an interpersonal context of human development would surely lead to misunderstandings. The guilt generated by human failure is not something static. Guilt can be the expression of inexperienced awkwardness in complex situations, a sense of inadequacy in demanding circumstances or the acknowledgment of moral failure.

Guilt means different things in different contexts. From the perspective of psychology, guilt represents wounded narcissism. One's drives toward desirable persons or objects are frustrated and negated by social forces that indicate under certain circumstances that these drives are unacceptable. The accompanying vulnerability due to negative social judgment leads to shame. Often this shame is emotional and intuitive but not fully comprehended. Thus the frustrated person becomes, in addition, wounded in his or her self-esteem as well as deprived of gratification.

In theology, the term guilt refers to conscious awareness of genuine fault. This is quite different from what was just described, since psychologically one can be the bearer of guilt without consciously knowing why. The further development of fault, the concept of sin, represents a conscious offense against love — either explicitly as an intentional offense against God or implicitly as an offense against others that is concomitantly an offense against God's commandments.[2] Great harm can be done by failing to recognize the nature of the phenomenon in a given life.

Religious psychologist Antoine Vergote has stated, "It is the paradox of Christianity that in proclaiming freedom from sin and deliverance from the law, it accentuates the demands of the law and sharpens the sense of sin."[3] During the early years of life, God is largely an abstract idea that represents the ultimate reason why prohibitions must be obeyed. It is noteworthy that most of the ten commandments are negative: "Thou shalt not. . . ." A God-image that is uniquely developed around the experience of prohibition will be a negative and forbidding one. At some important juncture in the psychological development of the adolescent, the church's proclamation "Go in peace, your sins are forgiven" will be received instead as the shocking and alienating judgment "You are a sinner!" For the message of God's compassion to detonate as good news, the listener must transform inadequate images of God into a symbol of life-affirming benevolence.

Primordial Struggle for Identity

Freud's account of the psychogenesis of moral existence recognized that the boy child's relationship with his mother was a kind of parable for the development of instinctual energies in the young child. Freud used the myth of Oedipus as a framework in which to interpret the blind groping of the child and youth for freedom.

The story goes this way: A small child intensely desires to remain attached to his mother, but as he grows up and discovers the stronger rival who is his father, he perceives the unattainability of possessing his mother as a love object. To the same degree that his unfulfillable wish for his mother is dangerous, to that same degree he builds defensive reactions to invest his frustrated energy in acceptable goals. If these goals are highly idealistic, the superego (the internalized voice of the parents) will be unrelenting in demanding not only relative goodness but perfection from the child.[4]

This oedipal narrative illustrates the ambiguity of the psychogenesis of the moral life. What children really want in their primitive urges is fusion with the mother (a nostalgia for the perfect union of the womb), while in fact the only way to please this inaccessible love object (the mother) is to undertake complex social development that distances them from their mother in terms of activity and affection. Children feel an unconscious guilt for wanting a forbidden love object and a conscious guilt for being unable to realize the perfection desired by the superego.

Oedipal development in the female child is structured differently. When the male child of five or six separates from the mother to begin developing a male-type identity patterned on father, brothers and/or other males, the female child of this age remains attached to the mother. As a consequence of staying within the world of women's dominant influences, girl children are excluded from the male society (where superior privileges exist) and can run the risk of internalizing a second-class status. Parallel to the classical Freudian account of oedipal forces, little girls come to know the frustration of their attachment to their fathers as inaccessible love objects and an experience of envy of males (father and brothers) for the superior status which society accords to them.[5]

Other accounts of psychological development during childhood and youth clarify this same problem of lack of coherence between inner impulses and external expectations. Piaget's studies of moral development, for example, describe young children (before age seven or eight) as characterized by forms of thinking called "heteronomy." At this stage, children perceive that their behavior produces disapproval from parents and other adults, but they can't understand why this is so. They are inclined toward authoritarian and severe judgments regarding how to punish offenders. Realistic perceptions of faults, moral consequences and responsible behavior only come gradually and usually not before the early teen years.[6]

Psychological reality, then, is marked by tremendous ambivalence. Guilt is an experience of failure to meet internal and external expectations. Guilt produces a tendency to withdraw and to rehash fantasies of failure rather than extend one's self to community and to the task of building the world. Frequently prolonged guilt motivates persons to escape from relationships that inspire guilt — to run away from what feels like a lost cause. Therefore, when children arrive at adolescence, they not only reject the frustration of submitting to what feel like irrelevant demands presented by authority figures, but they also reject the structure of a conscience formation built upon cultural goals extrinsic to their own understanding and feelings. The central point here is that successful conscience formation entails a movement beyond dependency and a willingness to assume responsibility for one's choices.

Cultural Ambiguities in Conscience Formation

To become a moral adult, one must make a transition beyond superego to ego identity, which is characteristic of the adolescent journey to adulthood. In our culture, many people make the psychological transition to ego identity without, however, being able to recognize that the genesis of their moral imagination was necessarily a process that had to begin with dependency upon the mother, to mirror the acceptable behaviors of the father and to internalize moral lessons from parents and culture. For no one is such a process of youthful moral education a perfect fit.

In our society, the entertainment industry often celebrates the inanity of parental moral values and the heroism of rebellion against authority. In many cases, the God-image and the church become identified with the dizzy mother and the impotent father of the TV comedy, and therefore the religious theme becomes negligible or negative. Often children receive little instruction from either parents or teachers concerning the meaning of God in their lives, and many times, church-going is at best an arbitrary expectation perceived as social duty and at worst an impenetrable nuisance that falls by the wayside. In either case, the transformation of God-imagery that should arise from personal religious experience will likely not occur or not be very positive.

The role of the church in such a cultural matrix is delicate: "By claiming that the confession of sin is a necessary condition for liberation from sin, Christianity exposes [people] to a morbid sense of guilt or, in clinical terms, to obsession neurosis."[7] Unless the experience of confession is coupled with an evangelical call to a new relationship with God that embraces the frailty and fallibility that persons have experienced in their weakness, then the experience of confession will celebrate merely an incapacity to meet the expectations of the father-figure God, the source of superego demands, and lead persons into a negative identity and the reinforcement of frustration.

Others can address parallel reasons why, in the church's ritual life, confession as such must be coupled with antecedent proclamation of God's compassion and with a community-supported process of being mentored within a network of positive examples and accepting fraternal love. Here in this psychological perspective we can affirm that someone on a journey to a healthy reworking of the God-image needs an invitation to an encounter of care and affirmation as the necessary condition for a healthy confession. The image of

God as *judge* is forcefully suggested by the ritual of the confessional box. How might the ritual experience of reconciliation suggest the more appropriate image of God as *prodigious father* (from the story of the Prodigal Son)? This transition from legal to familial imagery for God should also enable the development of other more sensitive God images, such as mother, friend, core of being, enabler or similar images.[8]

We have noted how the very evolution **Sexuality and Guilt**
of moral consciousness is related to the
child's sexual desire for the mother. Sexuality is at the heart of human fear and obsession with fault and guilt. In our Roman Catholic tradition, the magisterial teaching that there is no parvity of matter relative to sexual fault is the source of great psychological and moral confusion. (Traditional Catholic catechesis teaches that there is no venial sin in sexual matters. The majority of priests in pastoral practice, however, do not treat compulsive or habitual genital expression outside the context of marriage or self-gratification as matter for serious sin unless there are accompanying attitudes that suggest deep alienation from God. In this sense, sexual sin is frequently interpreted more symptomatically than it is categorically.)[9]

De facto we have caught people in a double bind. On the one hand, parents and teachers fear that talking about sex will conjure up dangerous sexual ideas and invest them with fascination; so they often virtually refuse to talk about sex at home or in the classroom. As a consequence, a child's curiosity goes unsatisfied and the child's questions go unanswered. In many cases, the first discourse about sexuality that children hear comes from television and from other children, and it is usually marked by a great deal of misinformation and exactly the tone of sensationalized excitement that one least desires to characterize sex education.

On the other hand, the church teaches that a person is responsible for serious fault regarding any infraction of sexual morality. Even thoughts about sexual actions are presented as dangerous and sinful. This massive culpabilization of sexuality can have pathogenic effects. Parents and authority figures give prohibitions against sexual activity in such a way as to intensify a religious climate of guilt. This suspicion that guilt colors any sexual expression generally impoverishes all affective life. As Vergote says, "It smothers creative forces and casts a shadow over life as a whole. What concerns us particularly here is that it produces a fearful and evasive style of religion, separating religion from the actual culture around it."[10] The fact that the mass media so often treat sex merely in terms of recreation and entertainment amplifies the confusion of a conscience struggling with issues of sexuality and identity.

The generation of free-floating feelings of guilt tends to repress the healthy passion for autonomy in all the domains of the young adult life — sexuality, aggressiveness, even freedom of thought. As a consequence, there develops a suspicion that moral goodness is identified with moral infantilism. To enter into autonomy and sexual intimacy is to risk transgressing the frontiers of safety and self-containment that the superego mandates. Reaching out to attain one's love object and striving to assert one's independence can be interpreted as perilous, even sinful.

The traditional Christian anthropology that treated intimacy as a symbol of transcendence has been lost or deformed. In fact, most young adults either do not know or do not respect the constraints on behavior that were formerly expressive of childhood or young adult sexuality. As to understanding the sacred (indeed sacramental) character of sexual intimacy, very few of today's youth have even heard the church's venerable traditions in this regard.[11]

To summarize some of the observations made so far, then, we can say the following: First, the quality of moral fault and moral experience is dependent upon psycho-social development. As Piaget has clearly indicated, the chief moral issue for the young child until the age of seven or eight is not clarity about the nature of the fault but a sense of having displeased people (especially parents) upon whom the child depends for love and affirmation.[12] The older child learns morality through cooperation. From eight to twelve or thirteen, the key moral issue is fairness and responsibility.

Children must be taught to be responsible, which principally means meeting social expectations and contributing meaningfully to the social enterprise of the school, the family and other primary human associations. The adolescent child is confronted with the integration of strong sensual and sexual feelings at the same time when issues of identity and intimacy surface as inescapable preoccupations. Adult moral agendas circle around commitment and care. It is easy to conclude, therefore, that moral questions must be contextualized by the psycho-social situation in which the moral agent finds himself or herself.

We may also say as a consequence of the above that no individual escapes some degree of psychic wounding. Missed opportunities, inappropriate or embarrassing initiatives, lack of responsiveness from objects of love or fascination and exclusion from desired opportunities are things that come into every life in one way another. "No wonder that when William Menninger was asked how many of us suffer from emotional illness he answered, 'One out of one of us.'"[13] This is not to say that psychological trauma is the only source of sin or moral fault. Yet whatever other genuine issues of morality may arise in a life, they will necessarily be affected by the developmental circumstances of a person's life.

Finally, we can see that for adult moral strength, the skills of intimacy and commitment are at the heart of an ability to "Do unto others as you would have them do unto you." The Golden Rule presupposes an ability to recognize the originality of the other rather than indulging in fantasies of resentment or idealization in our perception of others.[14] Additionally, the potential for commitment — making choices and deciding to become involved with others and then standing by those choices at all costs — lies at the very core of adult moral strength. It is also clear that both these virtues, intimacy and commitment, are especially fragile because of the very complications of psychogenesis that we described above.

One of the foundational ideas for Catholic moral ## The Qualities of a Moral Act

teaching is the description of the qualities of a "human act" as distinct from what might be called random acts performed by humans. Aquinas, early in his elaboration of the second part of his Summa, describes an act which is imbued with moral quality as "human." Such a moral action stems from intelligent understanding and considered freedom. This is familiar ground for anyone who has studied Catholic moral theology. The point of mentioning it here is that a significant consequence of Aquinas' teaching is that acts undertaken with insufficient understanding or diminished freedom are not fully responsible. Indeed, ignorance, constraint or violence can be causes for the loss of moral accountability. In such terms, we may say that the moral accountability of compulsive acts, fear-driven acts, stimulus-conditioned acts and similar examples would all be impeded by some lack of desired qualities of intelligence and freedom.[15]

Both psychologically and morally, a major goal for moral education is to render adult moral subjects aware of the lines of force that influence the moral environment. Some would claim that in today's mass-mediated world it is next to impossible for someone to have a deep level of understanding of one's motives and an unfettered freedom. Unlike them, we want to say that a person must learn to struggle with the influences of the conscious, subliminal and unconscious forces which are always interwoven within the fabric of our social and moral lives so as to develop the ability to respond with good enough understanding and good enough freedom.[16]

Classical Catholic moral teaching has always implicitly viewed adult morality as a developmental reality. The intelligence of the child grows through experience and exercise into a capacity for prudence and wisdom. People don't suddenly wake up when they are seven years old — at the "age of reason" — and simply have the wisdom of an adult. Prudence is an art as well as a virtue; it comes from learning, effort, exercise and decisiveness. Freedom likewise is the fruit of the consolidation of skills and discernment. One learns freedom by internalizing disciplines that allow the concentration of psychic energies to be applied to difficult and deeply desired goals.

Any person of any age can at times feel overcome by the powerful influence of others or by the forceful attraction of materialistic or hedonistic values in the popular culture. True freedom is the work of a lifetime. Yet good enough freedom and good enough prudence is something that gets better and better with experience and effort. Both psychology and theology therefore hold out as a goal the development of the consolidation of human intellectual and affective powers into the emergence of a person of decision, of virtue and of generative care for others.

This brief reflection upon the "human" act shows two things. First, people need presence of mind and determination to act as perpetrators of great good or great evil. Second, the great goal of the moral life is not avoiding mistakes but rather growing up into a responsible (knowing and free) person. Let me explore the tension between avoiding mistakes and achieving mature freedom a bit further.

Innocence or Integration

In psychology, we can see this tension expressed in part in a naive therapeutic hope for deliverance from psychic tension in the goal of catharsis. The fundamental idea here is that meeting compulsive unconscious forces in the company of a supportive therapist might allow one to look at the dark side of the self and rise above its alienating power. The problem with the notion of catharsis is that it is effectively static, turned back to some form of nostalgic state of well-being in the past.[17]

The great moral challenge of psychological development is to appropriate the full scope of one's psychic powers, described by Jung in terms of "individuation." Individuation aims at the formation of the "self" — a unique emergence of human psychic and social presence that draws into conscious interplay with one's companions, one's work and one's choices the energies that Jung names by the archetypes called "the shadow" and the "anima." I will not try to explain archetype theory here. The fundamental idea, however, is that a person takes responsibility to unify social elements of the self that have been formed in interpersonal dialogue with other dimensions of the self that have been residing beneath the surface of consciousness and which contain strong desires and powerful ideals.[18]

In a certain sense, individuation is the moment of "incarnation" of a whole psychic individual within a living bodily person. In this sense, we can see that catharsis as a goal is not good enough. Individuation is the authentic objective of a fully human life. Full humanity is won only at the price of confronting the truth of a personality that is both generous and selfish, loving and hateful, truthful and deceitful. To try to deny one's weakness — one's shadow — is to become its victim.

In some parallel way, something similar is true in the popular moral ideas that arise in preaching and catechesis. Understandably, when dealing with children, we can articulate the goal of innocence as a target for moral energies. With the very young, we want to protect them from learning too soon about the dark side of the human spirit and from entering too quickly into undisciplined self-expression that could be damaging to their moral evolution. Yet it is clear from the journey described in different ways within this paper that innocence can also be a form of denial of the need for the journey toward autonomy that is everyone's responsibility. Moral authenticity involves a journey of intellect and will toward prudence and freedom, as described earlier. This journey cannot be made without making mistakes. The goal is not *stasis* — that is, marching while standing in place. The reward of mature freedom comes not from going around painful experiences but from moving through them with conviction.

Bonhoeffer in his *Ethics* comments that in his view, a great moral issue for our day is truthfulness versus lies.[19] He goes on to observe that while truth-telling has always been a challenge for every age, in the twentieth century it has taken on a particular character. For the problem of untruth that is most threatening in our society is not persons uttering something other than that which is on their minds (telling lies), but the more radical problem of people living a life that is a lie.

The meaning, of course, is that people can stumble through life without sinking roots into the depths of their understanding and their freedom. Therefore in the routines of their existence, they express superficial personalities which are but a caricature of the full potential of their moral being. In some ways, we must ask seriously whether the church is on the side of lying or truth-telling, whether the church is asking for innocence or integration.

Are we able to describe the challenge of a moral life with such honesty that we include a believable account of the developmental journey which everyone who hopes to grow to wholeness will make? Do we allow our young to linger too long in the assumption that our fundamental concern for their morality is with their cheerful compliance with things the way they are, without clueing them in on their responsibility to renew the structures of church and society by their passionate reimagination of human and social goodness from their own gifts and new perspectives? Because we have done so poor a job with this in recent decades, our communities include many persons who are not able to function easily with the church's social or sacramental symbols.

Addressing Wounded Souls

We deal in our communities with three types of wounded persons: the alienated, the disaffected and the compulsively bound. (In addition, thank God, we also have people who have grown beyond alienation, disaffection or compulsion into community and cooperation.) By way of conclusion, let me address some remarks to each of the categories of these wounded souls in the light of the present discussion.[20]

The Alienated

I call *alienated* here people for whom traditional structures of morality and church teaching no longer have sufficient credibility to be taken seriously or to be taken as a rule of life. Alienation describes a personality no longer at home with the standard account of the community's story. Often, the alienated are precisely those who do feel themselves internally driven to the experiences of individuation and integration. For such persons the clarification of the categories of sinfulness or moral fault is extremely difficult.

I remember some years ago a notable Catholic laywoman saying that frequent confession, to which she was committed because of her belonging to the Young Christian Students movement, was painful because she had to keep rephrasing her sins until she came up with something that the priest recognized as sufficient matter for the sacrament according to the training that he got from his moral theology manual. We have to be careful not to lay legalistic trips on the alienated. The great good that we desire for them is for them to hear the word of God as a word of acceptance inviting them into a community that is the body of Christ. There is a place for them, even as they strive to tell the truth of the individuation.

Alienation is the experience of feeling excluded, misunderstood or unaffirmed by the very structures in which one participates. While many of the alienated may be poorly informed about church tradition or poorly catechized, the truth is that the church needs to hear from them about their experience. Sometimes the alienated are more perceptive about latent contradictions in church policy than are the ministers of the church. In any case, the alienated need to be welcomed under the tent of meeting, despite the burdens their cares may bring to the community.

The Disaffected

The great problem relative to the people I call bland or disaffected is that there is no passion in their lives. These are people who have perhaps kept religious practice at a level of simplistic sociological expectations. They go to church because other people expect them to. These are the people who sometimes say, "Father, just say the Mass, don't bother us with prophecy." More commonly, these are the people who have stopped going to church because the whole thing seemed pointless. The great challenge is to hold out before them a vision of transformation that genuinely excites and inspires them. The missing link for this group is that *they* are the body of Christ, *they* are offering themselves with the bread and the wine to the eternal God, *they* are the lifeblood of God's transforming presence in the world.

Those called disaffected here are missing the point of religious practice. How do we create conditions for them to have strong and positive religious experiences? Without some spontaneous dynamic of religious experience, they will not make the move toward belonging and commitment. Even if they do not consciously acknowledge a hunger for some strong religious experience, their pastoral ministers have to be astute enough to want that for them and to offer it to them.

The Compulsively Bound

The compulsively bound have little freedom. They have little self-respect and little feeling of power or ability to make an impact. Oddly, sometimes such people are in fact immensely talented and even superior producers. Some of the most remarkable scholars I have known have been people who felt compelled to work themselves to death in order to get attention or feel some sense of worth. There generally is a thick wall of insulation between their spontaneous feelings and the offer of affection and cooperation by others. Addictions to alcohol, drugs or other forms of sensual stimulation become a mainstay for many of these people, precisely because such powerful invasions of their senses offer them some symbol of self-affirmation. Yet in the very process of trying to affirm themselves, they often weaken and destroy themselves.

With the compulsively disabled, the avenue of liberation is the building of structures of belonging (like twelve-step communities such as Alcoholics Anonymous). Repeated events that bring people together and allow them to face their neediness in a context of acceptance and support creates a new world for them. When I was a religious superior, it was clear to me that some of the people with the strongest sense of psychological community in my province were recovering alcoholics who visited AA meetings three or even four times a week to receive the moral support and human affirmation that made it possible for them to rebuild their addicted lives.

The Power of Ritual

Ultimately, the great challenge for the church in renewing reconciliation is to develop ritual forms that will address the positive possibilities suggested in the discussion of treating the alienated, the ineffectual and the disabled. Can we bring truth, excitement and care to the assembly of the local church with such sensitivity and conviction as to cut through the defenses and the resistance of those who have spent years, perhaps, distant from the community?

Ritual has great power. One of its strongest qualities is its taken-for-granted characteristic. When we participate in rites, we defer to the structure of the rite. Much more could be said on this theme. I will limit myself to saying only that the enterprise of fine-tuning the rites of reconciliation and ReMembering has great potential for continuing renewal in the church now. Finally, it might be fitting to conclude with a comparison between psychological individuation and mystical awakening.

Each Christian is called by the baptismal vocation to become a friend of God and enter into a lifelong relationship of growth and friendship. Doing this is mysticism.

> In the mystical life one passes from one layer to the next in an inner or downward journey to the core of the personality where dwells a great mystery called God — God who cannot be known directly, cannot be seen (for no man has ever seen God) and who dwells in thick darkness. This is the never-ending journey which is recognizable in the mysticism of all the great religions. It is a journey toward union because the consciousness gradually expands and integrates data from the so-called unconscious while the whole personality is absorbed in the great mystery of God.[21]

It might seem inappropriate or ironic to be citing this great goal of mystical achievement in the context of addressing the needs of sinners, the broken and the alienated. Yet, in fact, only through a convincing portrait of the mystical goal (which is friendship with God) can we hope to awaken the passion and interest of people who have given up on the ecclesiastical enterprise. Only a goal of transcendent significance can unify the primal energies of a person's lifetime.

Throughout this paper, I have spoken about psychological and moral experience in terms of journey. The journey is fraught with many hazards, and no one makes it without wounds and fears and frustrations. Yet ultimately it is the destination that keeps us in motion. Christian belief holds out the promise that there is no one so wounded, no one so broken as to be unreachable by the mercy of God. That mercy is expressed in forgiveness spoken by the church and reconciliation with the church. Our task is to understand the geography of the journey and to offer travelers assistance truly appropriate to the challenges along the route.

For Pastoral Reflection and Response

"Our task is to understand the geography of the journey [of psychological growth and moral development] and offer to travelers assistance truly appropriate to the challenges along the route." This is a noble but daunting pastoral task that requires a working knowledge of how conscience is formed; of the relationships among psychological, moral and spiritual development; of the forms of companionship of the church; of the mystery of the human heart; and of the ways in which ritual expresses and deepens each of these realities. Some comments on each may help us reflect on our own pastoral ministry.

Dr. Philibert's wise and insightful portrayal of psychological and moral growth reminds pastoral ministers of all kinds to be constantly attentive to the complexities of these processes as we take our roles, assisting growth in Christ.

If the goal of moral education is "to grow into a responsible (knowing and free) person," what are the elements and methods of such formation? Perceptive understandings of a person's age, abilities, life experiences and socio-cultural situation are crucial. The experience and wisdom of the church and the wider human community, past and present, also are essential elements. But how shall we offer what we have to developing consciences? Will we speak in the "thou shalt nots" of the Commandments or, instead, in terms of the faith, love, honor, integrity, commitment and fidelity of the Beatitudes? Will we predetermine the questions and answers necessary for conscience formation, or will we allow growing persons to discover the values of our shared life in our great stories and in the witness of holy men and women who have preceded us in faith?

How we answer these questions very likely depends on how we understand the relationship between psychological, moral and spiritual development. Philibert traces the general development of a person from the infant's radical dependence on others for love and affirmation, to a childhood of cooperation through fairness and responsibility, to an adolescence which integrates strong sensual and sexual feelings with issues of identity and intimacy, to an adulthood of commitment and care. Psychologically speaking, this is the growth from superego to individuation; morally, this is the path of the maturing conscience, integrating the power for good and evil. In terms of spiritual growth, which is a necessary companion in this process, this is a movement from faith based on a narrowly defined image and understanding of God into a faith in the deeper and wider mystery of a God beyond imaging.

Of course, this path is straight and smooth for no one. There are obstacles at every turn: "missed opportunities, inappropriate or embarrassing initiatives, lack of responsiveness from objects of love, or fascination and exclusion from desired opportunities." All the more reason to ask: How do we honor the tortuous path of human growth and image God for people in our liturgy, preaching, catechesis and styles of ministry and in all the actions of the parish and the church (from bulletin announcements to papal encyclicals)? How do we name sin and evil, and the promise and hope of grace? How do we facilitate people's entering into the mystery of God ever more fully?

Do our programs reflect an understanding that conscience formation and spiritual development are lifelong processes, that there are periods of activity and dormancy, of advance and retreat in our friendship with God? It is hoped that each person has family who loves them and friends who appreciate them, especially in a society often in opposition to the values the gospel and the church propose.

The church too is a companion on this journey, an inspiring agent at every level of healthy moral growth. We possess the mission of proclaiming healing, hope, redemption, a future of mercy, forgiveness, inclusivity and reconciliation. With such good news we stand prophetically and compassionately with each person and in our society; we offer our experience and wisdom to all takers.

But the church and its ministers also can be, and have been, wounding agents, obstacles to moral maturity. It's a haunting question Philibert poses: whether the church is on the side of lying or truth-telling, whether the church is asking innocence or integration of its members.

As we think concretely about ministry with the people around us (or that we hope will be around us), who are the alienated, the bland or disaffected, and the compulsively bound or disabled, as Philibert describes them? What are their faces and stories? How can we listen to them in a way that signals that the church is on the side of truth-telling and integration? What are the clear and practical ways we can welcome the alienated in the truth of who they are and who we are? Can we take the necessary risks with compassion and humility? How can we offer the disaffected a vision that will touch and thrill their hearts, and inspire them to move more deeply into a faithful life? Can we provide the broken and bound the care, belonging and power they need to find healing and liberation? How do we also continue to nurture and support ongoing conversion in the healthy and strong members of the community?

There is a powerfully expressive and transformative role for ritual in the processes of psychological, moral and spiritual growth. It needs more study and experimentation. Our liturgical celebrations have their root and stem in the integration of life and faith, and they are meant to produce fruit in the world that will last. They name God, deepen the reality of God in us and in the world and give shape to the moral universe we call God's reign. But do our rituals, especially the rites of reconciliation, limit the names of God or reveal the multi-named God of mystery? Can they express and deepen hospitality, truth, hope, care and empowerment for the alienated, disaffected, disabled — and the strong and healthy? Our liturgies have the dangerous power to alienate as well as to welcome, to deaden as well as to excite, to oppress as well as to liberate. If the underlying spirituality is wounded or distorted, what kind of flower and fruit will it produce?

Pastoral psychology invites pastoral ministers to look at the journey each person takes in order to cooperate with God's grace, to acknowledge the social context of each journey, and to be wise about the many paths that lead to God's mercy in Christ. In faith it is a journey of friendship with God. At one and the same time, we walk the geography of the soul, discover it anew for ourselves, and we map it, guiding others through its valleys and over its peaks.

The oral responses given at the symposium by Clare Colella, director of Caritas Telecommunications, Diocese of San Bernardino, California, and Peter Ghiloni, then director of the Office of Prayer and Worship, Archdiocese of Milwaukee, Wisconsin, contributed greatly to these pastoral notes.

Are Anthropological Crises Contagious?
Reflexivity, Representation, Alienation and Rites of Penance

Fredric M. Roberts

James Lopresti's *Penance: A Reform Proposal for the Rite*[1] depicts a ritual response to the widespread experience of alienation from the church. This liturgical response to the present crisis is particularly fascinating to me as an anthropologist conducting participant observation research among liturgists as part of a larger project — American Catholic Ritual Life in the Post – Vatican II Era. For among the words that I might choose to characterize the dominant mood of many of the liturgists I have met are: beleaguered, embattled, embittered, tired, marginalized and alienated. On the other hand, I also might describe my own discipline, cultural anthropology, in much the same terms. But why should this convergence be a concern?

In this paper, I am going to suggest that over the last 20 years, major American liturgists have fruitfully drawn upon anthropology as a significant source of insight into both culture in general and ritual in particular. One reason these liturgists have found anthropology a congenial source of inspiration and support is the striking similarity between those who have been drawn to the academic study of liturgy and those who have become cultural anthropologists. In particular, both fields have attracted intellectuals profoundly alienated from the experience of life in mainstream Western culture and the irrational or immoral Others who seem to prosper in it. These alienated individuals have sought in their marginalized disciplines ways to construct for themselves (and their society) more meaningful definitions of Self. These definitions often are inspired by their "understanding" of exotic Others (remote either in time or space).

In cultural anthropology a growing recognition of this issue has led to a series of major crises seriously calling into question some of the discipline's core assumptions. Central to these crises have been the closely linked issues of *reflexivity* and *representation*. There has been an increasing awareness that anthropological findings and concepts all too often have unconsciously reflected the culturally constructed fears, desires, fantasies, alienation and power agendas of the Western Self as much or more than the lives of the non – Western Others under study. Serious questions have been raised about both anthropological field work (participant observation) and the construction of anthropological ethnographies and other texts (the primary ways in which anthropologists have mediated their experience and understanding of Others). Has the inherently dialogic/polyphonic character of the field work process and, more important, of culture itself, been dangerously suppressed by the construction of anthropological texts in the monologic, power-laden tradition of Western academic discourse?

Now, if one major reason liturgists have found anthropological insights so useful is that there are striking similarities between the Selves of liturgists and the Selves of anthropologists, it may be unavoidable that liturgists begin to ask themselves the sorts of questions anthropologists have been raising about their own discipline. And while the anthropological crises have been painful, the profound reflections and critiques they have prompted have led to an incredible increase in our level of Self-knowledge. This, in turn, has increased the likelihood of a more honest dialogue with and more accurate understanding of Others, both those who have been our "villains" and our "heroes." I believe that there may be a similar outcome in liturgy, allowing liturgists to deal more effectively with both their own alienation and the many other alienated Catholics who desperately need to be reached.

Obviously, the tasks of adequately defining and documenting major crises in two disciplines, much less relating the lessons to be learned from them to the task of healing the widespread alienation from the Catholic Church, are well beyond the scope of this short presentation. It will be necessary for me to state some tentative or preliminary observations and generalizations, asking you to consider them only provisional for the sake of my argument and open for correction, refinement and dispute. I also will focus on only a limited set of the relevant issues, ignoring or slighting ones that may be of equal or even greater importance. Although these are in some way serious failings, I see this as an opportunity to exemplify one of the key goals of the anthropology beginning to emerge from its crises: dialogization.

My goal is to begin a serious dialogue between anthropology and liturgy, with the ultimate hope of fostering dialogue or conversation among the variety of elements within the church alienated from one another. As Mikhail Bakhtin has suggested, true dialogue or conversation (which is at the heart of cultural pluralism) requires open-endedness, vulnerability and a lack of finalization. This assumes that interlocutors are not self-enclosed and deaf to each other but rather can, should and must be able to argue as well as agree.[2]

An Honest Story Honestly Told

Where to begin? Experienced teachers and writers all know that capturing the attention of the audience or readers is crucial. We also recognize that where we begin will influence to a great extent where we will end up. So this is a crucial decision of *representation.* Here I must choose my starting point from the material in hundreds of pages of field notes I have taken over more than a year of participant observation among liturgists in events ranging from intimate conversations around a dinner table to overflowing auditoriums at national conferences. In addition, there are my voluminous notes and clippings from a vast array of liturgy-related leaflets, articles, books and audio- and videotapes. These materials were aimed at audiences ranging from what Lopresti might term the liturgically "unawakened"[3] to members of the North American Academy of Liturgy, and they were produced by groups spanning the spectrum from advocates of immediate ordination of women priests to proponents of a return to the Tridentine Latin Mass.

Indeed, the anthropological analysis of the culture(s) of American Catholic liturgists implicit in this presentation will be my construction or representation, one out of any number of possible constructions or representations that I could have chosen to build out of the vast set of materials available to me. Indeed, this dynamic is not unique to my study but is now recognized by many anthropologists as being at the core of the discipline's work since its foundation. And the growing recognition of the centrality and power of cultural representation has been central to the crises in anthropology.

It is crucial to note that this has not led most anthropologists to abandon their claims to some sort of disciplinary expertise. The constructed nature of "culture" has not led anthropologists to discard standards of professional evaluation of their work in favor of a mindless relativism: "A culture is whatever any anthropologist says it is; so all constructions of a culture are anthropologically equal." On the contrary, it is increasingly clear to most anthropologists that their job is intellectually and morally more complex, demanding and problematic than was dreamed of by their professional predecessors. Clifford Geertz has summarized the job in a deceptively concise form: It is "a matter of how best to get an honest story honestly told."[4]

An honest story means having actually been there, among those Others, not just physically having shared Others' lives in such a way that you have "actually penetrated (or, if you prefer, been penetrated by) another form of life."[5] That, of course, always has been the goal of participant observation. However, it is now clear that such an honest story — an honest, intimate relationship with and knowledge of Others — requires honest knowledge of the Self. This is *reflexivity:* a knowledge of Self that encompasses not just a unique personality or a formal theory brought to the field but also the basic assumptions about the world (about the nature of reality) that the researcher brings from his or her own culture. These core cultural assumptions of Self have been instrumental in molding that unique personality, the theories available and chosen, and the very desire (often based in alienation) to leave the Self's home to learn about Others in general and a specific kind of Other in particular.

What do all these abstractions mean on the ground, in the daily work of anthropologists? They mean that we constantly ask searching questions of both Others and of our Self. For example, we are asking: Why am I really here? Why am I asking these people these specific questions? What questions am I not asking and whom am I not questioning? Who is rejecting me and whom am I rejecting? What am I not listening to in the answers I receive and in the questions Others ask me? What am I writing in my field notes and what am I leaving out? Ultimately, is there an intercultural dialogue going on here or, at best, two parallel monologues?

Additional Challenges

If reflexivity about our experience with and of Others has introduced some new questions about honesty into participant observation (an aspect of anthropology that has long been a key concern), reflexivity about writing about or representing the Other has raised issues of honesty in areas that anthropologists had seldom even considered problematic. It was generally assumed that telling a story honestly followed naturally from having an honest story to tell — in the above sense of a story based on "an honest, intimate relationship with and knowledge of Others." I already have introduced what is probably the most fundamental issue: recognition of the constructed nature of anthropological knowledge, particularly the constructed character of any anthropological interpretation or analysis of a "culture." Here, I just briefly will raise some additional concerns that I will later argue are of direct relevance to liturgists, particularly when they are dealing with the issue of alienation: "The pilgrim-cartographer challenge,"[6] the inherent quandaries of "translating Others for Others,"[7] and the questionable morality of the monologic representation of Others.[8]

As Geertz has pointed out, anthropologists have just begun to confront consciously the fact that their writing project is inherently odd: "constructing texts ostensibly scientific out of experiences broadly biographical" or, in terms that perhaps resonate better with the challenges faced by liturgists, trying "to sound like a pilgrim and a cartographer at the same time."[9] From all I have said above, it should be clear that anthropological research often involves a very deeply motivated personal quest or journey to meet the Other and to engage in a series of intimate Self/Other experiences. Yet anthropologists' authority back home (in and out of the academy) ultimately depends upon their ability to convince readers that they have not simply "gone native" but have retained the scholarly "objectivity" associated with "scientific" endeavors.

When this dilemma was consciously confronted in the past, the usual resolution to it was actually avoidance: The anthropologist would write two distinctive types of work. In one, often aimed at nonprofessional readers and seldom including a serious dimension of cultural reflexivity, the personal joys and sorrows, successes and failures of field work became the main story line, along with the personalities of specific Others. In the second type, the professional ethnography or article, the personhood or Self of the anthropologist and of specific Others were invisible (or appeared briefly in an introduction or epilogue). Colin Turnbull's pair of books about the BaMbuti Pygmies, *The Forest People* and *The Wayward Servants*, are early examples of this strategy.[10]

Probably inspired by the spirit of postmodern hermeneutics and the rapidly growing body of critical work in the sociology of knowledge that seriously questions the traditional view of "objectivity" even in the so-called "hard sciences," anthropologists recently have begun to face these challenges more directly and honestly.[11]

The second issue of representation can be summarized by the phrase "translating Others for Others." Obviously, one of the key challenges for an anthropologist is translation — learning to understand the nuances of the language of the Other being studied. Most anthropologists are skeptical of work done by a researcher who has only an elementary understanding of the Other's language or has to work through a translator. And even when working in one's own society with people speaking one's native language, the Others may be from a different social class, ethnic or religious group, or profession with its own jargon that requires a fair amount of "translation." The same words may have radically different meanings for the Others and the anthropologist. Sociolinguist Deborah Tannen's popular book, *You Just Don't Understand: Women and Men in Conversations,* has underscored dramatically some gender-based sources of such miscommunication in the United States.[12]

Even for anthropologists with the highest level of mastery of the Other's language, this translation problem inexorably reappears, in perhaps less obvious but just as significant forms, when it is time to transform their knowledge into texts aimed at still another set of Others, the implied or assumed readers. Obviously, anthropologists have to translate the pre-texts (e.g., field notes, interview transcripts, etc.) that will be incorporated into the final texts into the language of the readers. And all too often, the goal of elegance or smoothness of translation in the readers' language can result in serious distortions in the meanings of concepts. It also can result in the readers losing an opportunity for enriching their own Selves through knowledge of Others.

> [Let us] illuminate this point . . . by citing the eminent German translator Rudolf Pannwitz, who is quoted in that fine essay by Walter Benjamin entitled "The Task of the Translator." "Our translations, even the best ones, proceed from a wrong premise," says Pannwitz. "They want to turn Hindi, Greek, English into German instead of turning German into Hindi, Greek, English. Our translators have a far greater reverence for the usage of their own language than for the spirit of the foreign works. . . . The basic error of the translator is that he preserves the state in which his own language happens to be instead of allowing his language to be powerfully affected by the foreign tongue. Particularly when translating from a language very remote from his own, he must go back to the primal elements of language itself and penetrate to the point where work, image and tone converge. He must expand and deepen his language by means of the foreign language."[13]

In addition, the reflexive turn in anthropology has raised some serious questions about the influence of stylistic preferences on cultural translation. Scholars have demonstrated the astonishing degree to which the specific styles of thought and discourse highly valued by Western academics — *"this theoreticist or intellectualist bias"* — can seriously distort representations of Others.[14] For as Asad and Smith have emphasized: "What your style cannot easily accommodate, you leave out. Or if you do not leave it out, your style must diminish its significance."[15] For example, Karen Brown found that an accurate cultural translation of Haitian Vodou for an audience of Western anthropologists and religious studies specialists demanded that she construct a style of representation that acknowledged her own academic roots and her own Self (including its vulnerability and alienation) but, above all, remained honest to the very different style of the Haitian Others.[16] Retaining her own voice, she worked to include the Others' as well, for example, through an accurate representation of their storytelling, which is rooted in a view of memory and history radically different than that of the "Great Atlantic culture" of her audience. With the help of the extensive context Brown provides, readers willing to deepen and stretch their own experience of Others can follow the stories as they move "in a spiral fashion over and over the same ground when telling an important ancestral story" and can listen to a story told as a communal enterprise, with family members "twisting their word spirals in and around" each other's versions of a tale.[17] Above all, Brown struggled

> to create an intimate portrait of three-dimensional people who are not
> stand-ins for an abstraction such as "the Haitian People" but rather
> are deeply religious individuals with particular histories and rich interior
> lives, individuals who do not live out their religion in unreflective,
> formulaic ways but instead struggle with it, become confused, and some-
> times even contradict themselves. In other words, [her] aim is to create a
> portrait of Vodou embedded in the vicissitudes of particular lives.[18]

In this way she hoped to avoid the temptation enfleshed in the valorized cognitive and discourse styles of Western intellectuals "to drift off into logical dreams, academic bemusements with formal symmetry" that can seriously distort representations of Others.[19] Gananeth Obeyesekere also has warned against this temptation, specifically with regard to academic handling of myths and symbols:

> When a symbol is conventionalized, it loses its inherent ambiguity.
> Myths and symbols are part of the public culture; their syntactic looseness
> and ambiguity facilitates manipulation and choice. When a symbol is
> conventionalized it is deprived of its ambiguity, and ipso facto of its
> capacity for leverage and maneuverability. *One of the commonest occasions*
> *for conventionalization is when a popular myth or symbol is taken over by*

learned virtuosos and narrowed down and given limited and rigid meaning.
Their analytical status is quite different from that of symbol systems
on the ground, so to speak. *The "rational" explanation of symbols by academic*
anthropologists are of the same order: They also narrow the field of meaning
and produce a conventionalization of symbols.[20]

These concerns often are voiced by anthropologists working in the spirit
of Mikhail Bakhtin, who sought more honest anthropological representations
of Others. Bakhtin has been described by his major biographers as someone
who "did not fear being overwhelmed by the flux of existence. He was never so
afraid of being charged with theoretical inelegance that he felt compelled to a
premature systemization."[21] It is not surprising that anthropologists associate
Bakhtin with a position on representation radically at odds with the monologic
Western intellectual tradition, in which the author manipulates "the other not
only as an other, but as a self," i.e., reifies Others, transforming them from independent and never finalized consciousnesses into mere objects, supports or
props for the author's own story.[22] By contrast, Bakhtin considered it an author's
moral duty to include *"a plurality of independent and unmerged voices and con-*
sciousnesses, a genuine polyphony of fully valid voices."[23] And this moral obligation
is particularly powerful for the anthropologist, since an honest understanding
of Others ultimately must be rooted in the experience of really being there and
hearing and conversing with the genuine polyphonic voices of the Others.

The Case of U.S. Liturgists

What do these concerns
about reflexivity, representa-
tion, translation, monologue and polyphony, Self and Others have to do with
alienation in the church? Remembering that a basic element in the construction of anthropological knowledge of a culture is the author's choice of where
to begin the story, let me start at the national meeting of the Federation of
Diocesan Liturgical Commissions (FDLC), held at the Adam's Mark Hotel in
St. Louis in early October 1994. I was sitting with some of the delegates from
Region VI of the FDLC, desperately scribbling down notes of what the speak-
ers at the rostrum were saying and how they were saying it, as well as monitor-
ing how the audience of several hundred liturgists was responding.[24]

My research on American Catholic Ritual in the Post–Vatican II era and
particularly my entrance into the world of liturgists had been facilitated by two
people who became key informants: Sr. Marilyn Barnett, CSJ, and Dr. Nathan
Mitchell. Sr. Marilyn was director of the Office of Worship of the diocese of
Lansing, a cochair of Region VI of the FDLC, a member of the national board
of the FDLC and a member of the advisory board of the Notre Dame Center
for Pastoral Liturgy Associates, an organization of individuals with graduate
degrees in liturgy from that university. She had introduced me to Dr. Mitchell,

the associate director of the Notre Dame Center for Pastoral Liturgy and a prominent writer and lecturer on liturgical subjects.

Nathan and I quickly had become friends and collaborators, cowriting the summer 1995 edition of *Liturgy Digest,* which focused on liturgy and anthropology. Indeed, that collaboration was only possible because anthropology already had significantly influenced the thinking of a number of Notre Dame leaders in liturgical education and research, such as Dr. Aidan Kavanagh, OSB, and the late Dr. Mark Searle, as well as Dr. Mitchell. This was also readily apparent whenever I was first introduced as an anthropologist to Notre Dame liturgy graduates. Rather than being puzzled, they frequently would respond by reciting what was almost a litany of eminent anthropologists' names: Victor Turner, Mary Douglas, Clifford Geertz. Obviously, I was at the FDLC national meeting as a result of Notre Dame contacts, and much of my understanding of the liturgical world had been gained from talking with and observing Notre Dame liturgists. At the FDLC national meeting, I again was seeing many of the liturgists I had met at events in South Bend. It felt a bit like a reunion. Ironically, I felt more connected and welcomed than I normally do at the annual meetings of the American Anthropological Association.

Perhaps this welcome was particularly warm because I had come to offer my services as an ally from another discipline, an anthropologist also committed to many of the ideals of the liturgical renewal. This seemed like a refreshing change for liturgists, who were far more accustomed to constant attack from many sides. As I mentioned at the beginning, *beleaguered, embattled, embittered, marginalized* and *alienated* are words that I found very appropriate to describe the feelings of many of the liturgists I had met. (In turn, coming myself from a discipline often under attack from within and without, it felt very good to have people from another field look to us for some authority and insight.) As these terms certainly described the mood at the 1994 FDLC meeting, where individuals with major liturgical responsibilities from throughout the United States had gathered to voice publicly their concerns in a national forum, it seems an appropriate place to start introducing some of their voices into this account.

I'll begin at the top of the organization, with Father James P. Moroney, then chairperson of the board of directors of the FDLC. At one point in his lengthy and passionate address to the national meeting, Father Moroney recognized the sad reality of too few parishes using or even owning already approved liturgical books (like the *Order of Christian Funerals*), and he urged the delegates to find ways to touch the hearts of pastors ("most of whom are holy and overburdened people") with the "love of liturgy." Turning to introduce Bishop Donald Trautman, then chairperson of the Bishops' Committee on the Liturgy, Father Moroney described the bishop as "a man for whom we should all give thanks, for his love of liturgy, his courage in defending our art, his gentle heart. A true friend of liturgy!"

Bishop Trautman's own address was a powerful emotional appeal for liturgists to cling to that love despite trying circumstances: "Liturgists can lose hope, become tired from infighting and the tension of ministry. You can be bruised and battered. There will be the pain of rejection and misunderstanding. If we endure the cross for the gospel, we will share in the triumph of Christ!" The immediate context of the bishop's comments was what he described as "all the negative things of the past year."

Everyone in attendance knew that Bishop Trautman had been serving as an advocate to his brother bishops for many of their liturgical views during a particularly bleak period. In fact, the last national meeting of the FDLC in Rochester, New York, had taken place in the shadow of the decision of the American bishops (under great pressure from figures like Mother Angelica) to postpone a vote on the new translations of the sacramentary by the International Commission on English in the Liturgy (ICEL). Everyone at the 1994 meeting was painfully aware that the American bishops would soon again be debating the fate of these FDLC-supported ICEL translations. Attacks on ICEL's specific translations, as well as its principles for translation, were commonplace in many sectors of the American Catholic press.

Certainly, given "all the negative things of the past year," a high point in Bishop Trautman's address was when he affirmed and thanked the delegates for "struggling for full, active, conscious participation in the liturgy in a culture that scorns community and is rife with individualism and Lone Rangers and an entertainment mode of participation."

For the purposes of this paper, I wish to look closely at these few comments and in particular try to apply some of the anthropological ideas and concepts that have been discussed here. Obviously, I am singling out several small sections of only two of a large number of formal presentations at the FDLC national meeting, not to mention all the informal discussions that went on in restaurants, bars, hotel lobbies, elevators and airports. I feel that this is fair, at least for this type of brief presentation, since such selection is necessary in any anthropological construction, and it is a long established anthropological literary convention to focus analytical attention on what may initially appear to be an isolated or unusual event.

More to the point, what Bishop Trautman and Father Moroney said seemed strikingly representative to me of much of the liturgical talk that I have heard in so many settings, formal, informal, local, regional and national, since I began this research. And indeed, I can and will connect their comments with some of the major themes of Lopresti's *Penance: A Reform Proposal for the Rite.*[25] Finally, in order to indicate the tentative nature of my construction and to test the honesty of my choices, but especially to foster dialogue with the reader, I will be translating much of my analysis into questions, and these questions are not meant to be merely rhetorical.

A Dialogical Concept of the Liturgical Self

Underlying the entire notion of the Self/Other relationship as central to the process of anthropological construction of knowledge is a more generally applicable "dialogical concept of the 'Self'; identity is constituted not by essential characteristics but instead by a set of relationships to the Other, or whatever is *not* the Self."[26] For example, in *Portraits of "The Whiteman,"* Keith Basso has demonstrated that while anthropologists have been constructing the Western Apache as Other in relationship to their own Self, the Western Apache have, in their own distinctive genres and styles, been representing the Western Apache Self in relationship to the Anglo Other.[27] If we turn to the two brief excerpts quoted above (and Lopresti's *Penance*), what sorts of liturgical Self and Other are portrayed?

In the light of the comparison I have made between liturgists and anthropologists, I suggest that the pilgrim-cartographer challenge, or "constructing texts ostensibly scientific out of experiences broadly biographical" that is at the core of the anthropological endeavor, is also an inherent challenge for the liturgist Self.[28] On the cartographic side, the underutilized ritual books, such as the *Order of Christian Funerals* referred to by Father Moroney (as well as the embattled ICEL translations that were seldom far from the minds of those gathered in St. Louis), stake their claims to legitimacy and authority (official and otherwise) in great measure on arguments based in liturgical and historical scholarship. In turn, individual liturgists partly base their claims to personal authority and legitimacy at the national, diocesan or parish level on their in-depth understanding (often demonstrated through academic credentials) of those ritual books and the scholarship that underlies them.

Yet when in support of their interpretations of the ritual books liturgists construct their own texts — whether written (from parish bulletins to how-to books to scholarly tomes) or oral (from homilies to talks at national conventions to academic presentations) — they also call upon their pilgrim or experiential Selves as the source of authority and legitimacy. They represent themselves not only as experts in terms of scholarly or "scientific" knowledge but as Selves who have Really and Honestly Been There, had deep, personal, "authentic" and "valid" experiences of the liturgy, as Lopresti often characterizes them. And, in fact, a core element of such liturgical texts are representations of Self — attempts to *translate* the Self's pilgrim experience of the transcendent Other into terms human Others can understand and presumably wish to experience themselves.

Since this pilgrim dimension is so central to the liturgical Self, it is not surprising that Father Moroney and Bishop Trautman, as well as many liturgists, call on the "love of liturgy" both as the source of energy for proclaiming an unpopular prophetic message ("there will be the pain of rejection and misunderstanding") and as the emotion that must "touch the hearts" of Others (e.g., of "holy and overburdened" pastors) if liturgical renewal is to succeed. It is also this pilgrim dimension that leads liturgists, like Lopresti, to stress repeatedly that authentic experiences of ritual and liturgy are "enfleshed" and "embodied" (i.e., are not merely cerebral and cognitive).

There is absolutely nothing wrong with there being a pilgrim at the core of the liturgist Self. However, anthropologists' increasingly reflexive understanding of the critical implications of the pilgrim facet of their Self does raise some fundamental questions: Above all, if the Self "is constituted . . . by a set of relationships to the Other, or whatever is *not* the Self," how does the liturgical Self implicitly or explicitly represent the Other?[29]

Most obviously, the liturgical Self often is portrayed as alienated from and in opposition to both major elements of the church and a U.S. culture frequently represented as a radically immoral or irrational Other. When Bishop Trautman affirmed the liturgists for "struggling for full, active, conscious participation in the liturgy in a culture that scorns community and is rife with individualism and Lone Rangers and an entertainment mode of participation," he was repeating, almost verbatim, a construction of the American Other by liturgists that I have heard and read innumerable times. Actually, Lopresti's whole reform proposal of the *Rite of Penance* assumes the existence of a powerfully countercultural faith community. Indeed, for Lopresti the presence of such a community seems a necessary prerequisite for the Other to move from the experience of alienation to the experience of authentic and valid participation in the liturgy (implicitly assumed to have been experienced by the liturgical Self of the author and his sympathetic readers).[30]

Let me make this clear: Like most anthropologists, I am alienated from many key elements of my construction of my society's culture. In fact, Bishop Trautman's description of American culture is one that students probably hear all too often in introductory courses in anthropology. But, like most seriously reflexive anthropologists now working in their own society, I wonder whether such a representation of the Other next door (or even in my own house) is based in an honest story. Have I actually been there, and not just physically, among those many different types of Others in my own home society? Have I shared those nearby Others' lives in such a way that I have "actually penetrated (or, if you prefer, been penetrated by) [that close but distant] form of life"?[31]

Obviously, liturgists and other pastoral ministers interact with many of these Others; when liturgists get together, their conversations are peppered with anecdotes or horror stories about run-ins with such Others. But have they penetrated their lives deeply enough so that they can tell an honest story about the Others, honestly represent them as the Others? I seriously wonder. For, reviewing my experience with liturgical writings and presentations, I am struck by the conspicuous absence of *"a plurality of independent and unmerged voices and consciousnesses, a genuine polyphony of fully valid voices."*[32] The silence of the Others' voices is deafening once you try to listen for them.

The tragic loss of insight about the worship life of Others resulting from such a deafening silence is underscored in a study by Robert Orsi.[33] Orsi analyzes devotion to Saint Jude Thaddeus, patron saint of hopeless causes, which began in South Chicago in 1929. While he considers the official discourses on the devotion, he goes beyond them to consider the Other voices he heard when conducting interviews with the devout and reading responses to questionnaires distributed during a novena at the shrine in 1987.

On the basis of these other sources, he labels a key section of his study "Whose Voice? The Dialectics of Popular Religion." There he turns to the usually absent voices to consider "the question of how people *live in, with and against* the discourses which they inherit."[34] Because he listened to those voices, he can provide many examples of ways in which women actually did resist the official and male view of devotions with a different type of discourse, and can demonstrate how these women created "networks of support and assistance among their female relatives and friends similar to those their mothers and grandmothers had relied on in the transition from the old world to the new."[35] As Orsi argues:

> Acting within this network and in relationship with the gentle, powerful, attentive companion saint, women felt themselves to be empowered in new ways. They broke off relationships with "mean" boyfriends, rejected unwanted medical treatments, passed difficult qualifying exams of different sorts, and confronted family crises with newfound confidence. Throughout the 1940s and 1950s, for example, when the official voices of devotional culture were decrying women's return to work, the devout found in their relationship with Jude the strength and confidence to look for, secure and keep their new jobs.[36]

Indeed, Orsi suggests that listening to these Other voices can lead to a new understanding of devotionalism, not only as the place of gender construction but as the privileged site of gender contestation in American Catholic culture. Devotional culture was polysemous and polyvalent. Women not only "discovered" who they were in the dense devotional world that developed through much of this century in the United States but created and imagined themselves, manipulating and altering the available grammar of gender. Religious traditions must be understood as zones of improvisation and conflict. The idea of a "tradition" itself is the site of struggle, and historically situated men and women build the traditions and counter-traditions they need or want as they live. Finding meaning in a tradition is a dialectical process: Women worked with the forms and structures available to them, and their imaginings were inevitably constrained by the materials they were working with. Still, through the power of their desire and need, and within the flexible perimeters of devotional practice, they were able to do much with what they inherited.[37]

I have quoted Orsi at length because certain types of devotions are of particular concern to the liturgists I have met. Might the current construction and representation of the devotional Other be altered, at least in part, by taking into account the polyphony, polysemy and polyvalence that Orsi considers? Might the representations of those devotional Others (often as individualistic and medieval in their magical thinking) at least be less alienating to the latter if they felt that their voices had actually been heard?

It is particularly ironic to me that while contemporary liturgists often do not listen carefully to the voices of the Others all around them, a number of medieval social historians influenced by cultural anthropology and studying liturgy or liturgy-related subjects[38] have made extraordinary efforts to reconstruct out of crumbling documents and artifacts the voices of the many Others who have been dead for hundreds of years. These social historians obviously feel that an honest representation of the experiences of the historical Others requires that more voices be recognized than those official voices that have dominated historical accounts.

Inspired by cultural anthropology, these social historians also have attempted to construct in-depth accounts of the culture of the historical Others. They have recognized that liturgical symbols and rituals can only be honestly interpreted and represented when placed within the incredibly complex context in which the Others experienced them. These studies have direct implications for contemporary liturgists.

Take as an example the work of only one of these eminent social historians. Caroline Walker Bynum's illustration of the complexity of the notion of the individual in the twelfth century and how it influenced religious practices suggests that liturgists take a more nuanced look at individualism in twentieth-century America.[39] Bynum's study of the many implications of a particular cultural construction of the body in the High Middle Ages suggests that liturgists clearly must consider the many and unexpected ways in which contemporary Others may hear and understand the emphasis on the Body of Christ that has long been central to liturgical renewal.[40] Bynum's study of "The Religious Significance of Food to Medieval Women" certainly suggests that liturgists should understand attitudes toward the eucharist in relationship to the variety of contemporary cultural constructions of food and eating.[41] Finally, though Bynum's "Critique of Victor Turner's Theory of Liminality" explicitly relates to stories of women saints during the Late Middle Ages, it clearly suggests that a key anthropological concept often used by liturgists today (liminality) may, in fact, incorporate unwittingly a serious gender bias (i.e., it may be built on assumptions that may be appropriate for male Self but not necessarily for female Other).[42]

More generally, in light of the issues raised above, can liturgists truly claim to evaluate honestly the quality (authenticity or validity) of these Others' participation in the liturgy? Do they honestly feel that they know how these

Others have experienced the liturgy? Have liturgists' representations denied the validity of Others' forms of participation and deep experiences of the liturgy — and thus deeply alienated the Others — because liturgists have unconsciously assumed that to be authentic the Other must be just like the Self (an attitude that anthropologists normally label as ethnocentrism)? When Mother Angelica told a mean-spirited joke implying that liturgists are more irrational than terrorists, did liturgists almost become obsessed about it because there was possibly a small grain of truth in the comparison (like terrorists, liturgists sometimes appear to be constructing an Other denied of the true depth and complexity of real humans)?

Finally, one of the most potentially alienating elements in liturgists' relationships with Others may stem from another key aspect of cultural representation, insensitive translation, and ironically, in this case insensitive translation of key elements of their own liturgical self. Interestingly, James Clifford, one of the seminal figures in the crisis in anthropological representation, wrote his dissertation about an analogous issue, the way in which Christian missionaries have translated central aspects of their faith to Others from radically different traditions.[43] In particular, Clifford focused on the extraordinarily skilled cultural translation efforts of Maurice Leenhardt (1878–1954), an eminent French Protestant missionary-anthropologist who lived for many years in New Caledonia in Melanesia.

For example, Clifford relates how Leenhardt "finally arrived at a term that would express 'redemption'":

> Previous missionaries had interpreted it as an exchange — an exchange of life, that of Jesus for ours. But in Melanesian thinking, more strict equivalents were demanded in the exchanges structuring social life. It remained unclear to them how Jesus' sacrifice could possibly redeem mankind. So unclear was it that even the *natas* [indigenous Melanesian pastor-evangelists] gave up trying to explain a concept they did not understand very well themselves and simply employed the term "release." So the matter stood, with the missionary driven to the use of cumbersome circumlocutions, until one day during a conversation on I Corinthians 1:30 Boesoou Erijisi used a surprising expression: *nawi*. The term referred to the custom of planting a small tree on land cursed either by the blood of battle or some calamity. "Jesus was thus the one who has accomplished the sacrifice and has planted himself like a tree, as though to absorb all the misfortunes of men and to free the world from its taboos." Here at last was a concept that seemed to render the principle of "redemption" and could reach deeply enough into living modes of thought. "The idea was a rich one, but how could I be sure I understood it right?" The key test was in the reaction of students and *natas* to its provisional version. They were, he reports, overjoyed with the "deep" translation.[44]

Clifford goes on to suggest that as a result of this "deep" translation process (which is strikingly reminiscent of Pannwitz's understanding of translation described earlier):

> Often enough, Melanesian terms seemed to express the elemental meaning of the Bible more truly than the French or the Greek, both of which were less concrete tongues than the original language of the gospels. Thus Leenhardt's intercultural translation was more than a simple scriptural exegesis. His "primitivizing" of the gospel restored to it a rich, immediate context and concrete significance.[45]

It may seem that such deep translation is not necessary when communicating with Others from one's own society, people who apparently speak the Self's language. But, as anthropologists now recognize, ignoring more subtle translation problems like social class differences and the "theoreticist or intellectualist bias" can result in unintentional but equally alienating representations. Might it be well worth the effort to discover what Others think liturgists are saying when they continually talk about individualism, community, enfleshing, embodying, the assembly, the people, and full, active, conscious participation? This dialogue with Others might, indeed, lead to a series of deep translations that would not only remove some unintended sources of alienation but enrich liturgists' understanding of these key elements of their own Self.

For Pastoral Reflection and Response

Cultural anthropologists, social historians and other social scientists help us listen more respectfully and attentively to life and help us seek out and learn from Others around us or in our past. They are dialogue partners who can help us explore the human dimensions of brokenness, alienation and separation from the community, unearth underlying causes or patterns of alienation and examine practices of excommunication and their meaning. And what do the social sciences have to say about the processes of reintegration, healing and reconciliation? Where are the places in societies, past or present, where these processes have occurred or are occurring? What can we learn from these?

These are the kinds of questions we might expect an anthropologist to address around our topic of reconciliation, but Dr. Roberts chose to enter the discussion by a different door. Rather than bringing forth data that cultural anthropologists and social historians can provide, he raises the prior question of how such data is gathered, represented and interpreted. How do we "construct" or represent the Selves and the Others who are part of human processes of alienation and reconciliation? Can liturgists, homilists, catechists, penitents, musicians, artists, pastoral ministers — indeed, the church — engage in true dialogue to get "an honest story honestly told"? How can we tell the story of God's grace, mercy, judgment and justice, forgiveness and reconciliation in the face of human sin and virtue, evil and love, injustice, brokenness, oppression and hope?

We begin with the "reflexive Self," which may take the form of the individual believer, liturgist, composer, bishop, pastoral minister or even parish trying honestly to represent the Other. And an "examination of conscience" begins:

Why am I (the Self) really here?

Why am I asking the Other these specific questions?

What am I not asking? Whom am I not questioning?

Who is rejecting me? Whom am I rejecting?

What am I not listening to in the answers I receive and in the questions Others ask me?

How have I contributed to the alienation of the Other?

What is my own alienation within myself, the dangerous rift between my intentions and my actions?

Have I actually been there, and not just physically, among the many different types of Others in my home society?

Have I shared the nearby Others' lives so as to penetrate (or be penetrated by) that close but distant form of life?

These questions are not cold or objective; they are the first step in a true conversation that is open-ended, vulnerable and lacking in finalization. The Self steps into the pulsing heart of the matter, whether it is a confessor presiding at Rite I of the *Rite of Penance,* a parish grappling with clergy misconduct, a community or neighborhood discerning race relations, a parish council deciding on a church renovation, or any number of other Selves seeking reconciliation.

The Self is always a "pilgrim-cartographer" trying to bring forgiveness, healing and liberation while at the same time seeking those graces for one's Self. Thus, as liturgists and other pastoral ministers, we will have to keep seeking ways to gather and represent "the plurality of independent and unmerged voices and consciousnesses." Again, some examination questions:

Can we, who are ourselves alienated from the predominant culture and from elements within the church, claim to evaluate honestly the authenticity and validity of Others' experiences of life, church, liturgy, God?

Have we denied the validity of Others' experiences of brokenness, sin, oppression, evil, alienation?

Do we have in place opportunities and structures for hearing the polyphony of voices?

Are we willing to remain open and vulnerable, knowing that there are still more voices to be heard and that listening is never done?

One test of our representation of the plurality of voices is whether the 1973 *Rite of Penance* "translates Others to Others." Does it translate a reconciling God or a reconciling church to an individual sinner or to a sinful world? Does it translate the sinner to God and the church? Does it translate liturgical ritual to honest life stories, and vice versa? Studies show that 60 to 75 percent of American Catholics celebrate penance only once a year or never[1] and that 25 to 40 percent are at Mass on a given Sunday[2] (although they also now affirm the eucharist as their primary form of sacramental reconciliation[3]).

But if men and women of faith are not celebrating in the church, they are celebrating in ways more directly related to their stories: in AA groups or in support groups for victims of abuse, for women, for gays and lesbians, for the divorced and separated, and so on. Participation in advocacy and action groups organized around human service and social justice are other ways people seek and find support, healing and community, and work toward wholeness and, indeed, salvation. What can we learn from this? What does it tell us about where the need is? And are we as a church open enough and lacking enough in finalization to engage these Others in honest conversation? How will this transform our liturgies and pastoral ministry, and how can our liturgies and ministry transform human experience?

The reality of alienation and reconciliation touches every person and culture. Consequently, the mystery of reconciliation as God's activity and gift makes it the ongoing ministry of the whole church. It belongs to the community of believers, to church leadership, to pastors and their associates, to all the ministers within the church: liturgists and musicians, catechists and teachers, poets and artists, those in counseling, health care and social work, and many others. The work of reconciliation belongs to the whole body.

And so we return to the core question Dr. Roberts raises: How do we best get an honest story honestly told? Perhaps the church (as "pilgrim-cartographer") needs to be much more energetic about "naming grace"[4] rather than naming sin, affirmation rather than accusation. Does the work of reconciliation start at a place different from what we have imagined?

The oral responses given at the sumposium by Eleanor Bernstein, CSJ, director of the Notre Dame Center for Pastoral Liturgy at the University of Notre Dame, and Jerry Galipeau, director of liturgy and music at St. Marcelline Church, Schaumburg, Illinois, contributed greatly to these pastoral notes.

Paul's 1 Corinthians on Reconciliation in the Church Promise and Pitfalls

Margaret M. Mitchell

Our goal in this Bible reflection is to look at Paul's ecclesiology in 1 Corinthians and to lift up and explore its profound legacy to the church's understanding of itself in the context of the dynamics of reconciliation. 1 Corinthians is Paul's fervent attempt to reunite a church torn apart by factions. In that process, the apostle draws upon contemporary political lore and commonplaces to paint what is perhaps the most eloquent call for ecclesial unity in the New Testament. At the same time, his strategy raises significant questions for contemporary churches about the nature of compromise in the pursuit of concord, the extent of conformity required for unity, and the social and power dynamics involved in such negotiations. This dilemma is not one which Paul himself created, but it is the dilemma inherent in his call for unity in 1 Corinthians, which remains alive and well into this generation and beyond. The reason for this, as Paul understood so well, is that the church is a social/political body that faces the same conundrum all such bodies face: how to form a unified group from varied, isolated individuals? This fundamental issue of human political theory and practice is also the fundamental issue of Christian practical ecclesiology.

Because the focus of 1 Corinthians is internal church unity, we shall be looking at the phenomenon of reconciliation though that lens. I invite us all to think and imagine how our learning from this text might apply to wider global, political contexts, and even smaller, personal contexts which require reconciliation.

An Overview of 1 Corinthians

Sound exegesis demands that we first examine the historical context of this letter, asking when Paul wrote it and why. (My exegetical treatment of 1 Corinthians depends throughout upon my detailed study, *Paul and the Rhetoric of Reconciliation,* to which I refer the reader for full documentation.[1]) From the outset of 1 Corinthians (1:10–13), it is clear that Paul wrote the letter to address the problem of factions or divisions within the church, a purpose which remains constant throughout the letter (see also, for instance, 3:4f; 11:18; 12:25). Thus one immediate thing we learn is that factions in the church go back to the very beginning, to within 20 years of the death of Jesus (a fact which may both console us in our sense of decline and worry us that contentiousness is our permanent birthright). Recent Pauline scholarship has concluded that there was likely a range of factors responsible for and contributing to the Corinthian divisions (not unlike most contemporary church conflicts),

including ethnic diversity, economic disparity, geographical and sociological differences (separate house churches), disputes about gender roles, allegiances to
different missionaries, and theological disputes.

Paul, who had founded the church at Corinth (2:1–5; 3:6, 10), writes later
from Ephesus in Asia Minor, where he has been the recipient of a remarkable
number of Corinthian communiques: oral reports from Chloe's people (1:1) as
well as other unnamed oral reports (5:1; 11:18); a letter from some Corinthians
(7:1); and a delegation of prominent Corinthian Christians (16:17–18). Why
did all these Corinthians take the voyage across the Aegean to Ephesus or the
lengthy land-route via Macedonia to visit Paul? In my judgment, the variety of
contacts to Paul itself testifies to a divided church, with representatives of different groups appealing to Paul to confirm that they are right on the various
issues of contention. Thus Paul's in-box and appointment calendar are filled —
with Corinthians appealing for his support for their side of the conflict.

So, what is Paul the pastor to do? First, he is compelled to make a long-
distance diagnosis of the situation. He comes to the decision that it is the spirit
of divisiveness itself which is the main problem, more important than any single subject or practice that is in dispute. Based upon the diagnosis, he writes a
letter which urges unity above all other considerations. Paul constructs that
response, which we know as 1 Corinthians, with great care. The letter begins
with a direct appeal in 1:10, which functions as the thesis statement to the
whole letter: "I urge you, brothers and sisters, through the name of our Lord
Jesus Christ, to all say the same thing, and not let there be factions among you,
but be reconciled in the same mind and the same opinion" (my translation).
Paul's major appeal is for Christian unity in the single name of Jesus Christ
(1:2, 10, 13) in opposition to any other name or banner which individual
Corinthians might claim. The unity for which Paul appeals is urgent and deep,
expressed in four parallel and powerful locutions, positively and negatively: "say
the same thing" (a metaphorical statement for "agree"), let there not be factions
among you ("rips," "tears," a violent image of the Body of Christ being torn
limb from limb [1:10, 13; 12:25]), but be reconciled (a medical term used to
refer to the resetting of dislocated joints) in the same mind (a term which calls
to mind the Greek word for political unity, homonoia) and the same opinion
or judgment. The Christian unity Paul appeals for is organic, and holistic — in
body, mind, name and judgment — and is rooted christologically, as he states
again explicitly in 2:16: "We have the mind of Christ."

Paul follows up this thematic statement with four chapters centered on
unity itself as a general consideration before he turns to any of the things over
which the Corinthians are contending. In this opening section (1:18 — 4:21)
he is very careful always to award praise and assign blame to the entire church
as a whole, thus trying not to reify the factions by treating them separately. He
is severe in his critique of factionalism and warns that anyone who destroys
God's temple (the church, through divisive activity) will be destroyed by God

(3:17). Only after this prelude does Paul venture to discuss the actual issues over which the Corinthians are divided (in chs. 5 – 15). He begins with boundary issues of the way the church should and should not relate to the outside world and culture (chs. 5 – 10), then turns to internal church issues related to worship and liturgy, which has been the theater of disputation (chs. 11-14), and lastly takes up the topic of resurrection of the Christian dead, which has been questioned by some Corinthians (ch. 15).

Because his goal is the reconciliation of the church, Paul writes carefully on these specific problems and tries to mediate between opposing positions as much as possible. For this reason his precise advice is hard to discern as, for instance, on eating meat sacrificed to pagan idols, where one cannot pin down a Pauline "yes" or "no." Instead his answer is a qualified and careful "it depends" (compare 8:1–13 and 10:14—11:1). Some have asked if he does not "waffle" in some of these sections, especially given his own voluntary self-characterization in 9:19 – 22: "I have been all things to all people." This is a description of his mediatorial role: Above the factions he "is pleasing to all in everything, not seeking my own advantage, but that of the many, so that they might be saved" (10:33). These arguments and others which Paul uses to appeal for unity above all else are rooted in the Greco-Roman culture which Paul and the Corinthians share, for unity and factionalism are, of course, common political problems which had been given extensive attention.

Seven Arguments for Reconciliation in I Corinthians

Paul cast his argument for church unity in terms that would have been recognizable to the Corinthians from their wider culture, but he Christianized those arguments and gave them a specific application (or reapplication) to their church situation. For our task — to analyze the dynamics of the appeal for reconciliation — we will briefly examine seven arguments that Paul uses for unity in 1 Corinthians which are also found in other speeches and letters from Greco-Roman antiquity in which a philosopher, politician or teacher tries to convince a group to seek the course of unity over division. We shall briefly assess the positive and negative repercussions of each.

Ones

These are the thing the group has in common. Paul tries to persuade the Corinthians to be unified by stressing the things that they share: one calling (1:24–26), one God (8:6), one Lord Jesus Christ (8:6), one Spirit (12:13), one confession of faith (12:3), one baptism (12:13), one eucharistic celebration of one body of Christ (10:17), one common language (ch. 14), one set of common traditions (11:2; 15:1–3). The term *heis* ("one") is used a remarkable 31 times in the letter.

Surely Paul is right that anyone who tries to appeal for group unity must draw upon or create in that group a corporate consciousness, which must be rooted in the things that hold them together. A healthy, solidified group must know what it is that "makes them one," and those "ones" must be things that truly matter. On the other hand, this leads us to ask some key questions: What are the limits to "oneness"? Must Christians wear the same clothes? Must they vote for the same politicians? share the same lifestyle? listen to the same music? raise their children the same way? pray the same way? hold to the same doctrines? This dilemma is especially pointed in the language Paul uses in 1:10: "Say the same thing," have the "same mind" and the "same opinion." What are the limits to this? How does individuality fit in here? We can compare this with the different image of the chorus: Each person sings a different note, tone or melody line, but it is in the blending of the different voices that a euphonious, harmonious sound is produced, one that is more beautiful than any single voice. If the emphasis is on "saying the same thing," how does the church decide when someone is "saying something so different" that they are a tear or rip in the body of the church? What are the limits to oneness, to sameness? On the other hand, what are the limits to inclusivity? What happens to Christian identity when the "ones" get fewer and fewer?

The Social/Political Unit as a Body

This is the most common appeal for concord in Greco-Roman antiquity, here in its Christianized transformation by Paul as "the body of Christ" (12:12:31; cf. 6:15). There is an old, famous fable of the Roman statesman Menenius Agrippa, who in a time of faction exhorted the plebs to end their sedition by telling them the parable of the body in which the hands refused to feed the belly, with the result that the entire body (hands included) died. (As the story goes, the plebs were convinced and went back to work.) The customary points of the body metaphor for the political unit are that the whole body shares the same health, the same definition of advantage; there is a proper distribution of gifts and functions in the body, with an inbuilt design for unity in diversity; and common "membership" in the body is defined by suffering and rejoicing in common. Paul's Christian version of the body metaphor in chapter 12 includes all of these elements and is incorporated in this letter explicitly to combat division: "God blended the body giving greater honor to the lesser member so that there might not be faction in the body" (12:24–25).

Paul's body of Christ is still today the most well-known and favorite ecclesiological image, for its richness, its power and the sense of belonging it instills and promotes. At the same time, the body metaphor is inherently hierarchical: Who is a head? Who is a fingernail? Remember, the plebs were the hands, but the senate was the belly that received the benefit of all their work! Further, it asserts divine legitimation of the social order (12:18), which Paul accepts. You are a fingernail, God intended you to be a fingernail, stay a fingernail. He acknowledges that there are weaker and stronger, and honorable and less honorable parts of the body, and he tries to relativize these categories by arguing that all are necessary to the body and all share its collective honor. At least theoretically (and surely eschatologically [15:42f]), God reverses the hierarchy (12:24). But does this adequately deal with the possible negative uses of the body metaphor to ordain the status quo? A second question we might ask about the body of Christ metaphor is about its inclusivity. One must recognize that it is a "boundary metaphor"; that is, it serves to separate the church (the baptized [12:13]) from outsiders. It is an insiders' image. Could this perhaps be a limitation in an ecumenical age? Do all who employ the body metaphor for its positive elements recognize these possible limitations?

The Building as an Example of Concord

Paul's second image for the church, as God's building, is found throughout 1 Corinthians (1:6–8; 3:9–17; 8:1; 10:23—11:1; 14:3–5, 12, 26; 15:58; 16:13; cf. Mark 3:24–25 and pars.). Here the Greco-Roman commonplace (which is nicely phrased in the gospels in Mark 3:24–25: "a house divided against itself cannot stand") is applied to the church, God's building, which is also the temple of the Holy Spirit, on the firm foundation which is Christ. Paul's appropriation of this metaphor for the church is especially striking when we remember that in the ancient church, there were no actual church buildings. The consequences of this communal metaphor are that the members of the building must be strong, unwavering and unchanging, in order to build up the building instead of allowing it to totter and fall, and ultimately be destroyed by inner division (15:58), i.e., structural damage.

What good is the church to the world if it cannot stand on its own two feet? Surely, stability remains absolutely crucial if the church is to do its work in the world. Paul's architectural metaphor also makes way for new generations to "build on" the work that has come before, and it has an active component in that very work, which can be more than maintenance of the inherited physical plant. And there is another important aspect of this architectural metaphor for the church. In 3:12 Paul inventories the different kinds of building materials. All individuals bring different gifts, different lives, which are different construction materials for the church building. Yet all are not of the same quality, and all are not equally valuable in each place in the building. For example, silver and gold would make disastrous structural beams, while concrete doesn't do much for windows! Who is "the wise construction engineer" (3:10) who helps to deploy the church's natural resources in a fair and commonly advantageous manner? On the other hand, there is the matter of taste. Which is prettier and more fitting to the building of the church: gold leaf or simple wood? The strongest buildings we have are concrete bomb shelters, prisons and hospitals — uniform and secure, yet boring and prefabricated, hardly expressive of the living human (let alone divine) spirit. And no one lives there! Are strength and unity the only considerations for an architect (or a pastor)? Surely the church must be firm and secure, but can it also take some risks, make some architectural experiments, as it seeks to live out its destiny as the receptacle of the Holy Spirit?

Love

In 1 Corinthians, Paul constantly appeals to love as the principle of social cohesion, the great unifier (4:21; 8:1; 12:31b –14:1a; 16:14, 24). Throughout this letter, love is not a rapidly beating heart but a concrete action for unity. It is the mortar between the bricks of the Christian building; it is the sinews in the body (to develop Paul's images beyond what he himself says, but in spirit with him). In fact, in 8:1, love is what "builds up." Love also seeks the common advantage, not its own (13:5; cf. 10:23f). Love is the antidote to factionalism for Paul (as it was for Hellenistic Jewish and Greco-Roman writers of his time). We can see this in each of the epithets that are applied to love in the famous "hymn to love" in 13:4 – 8a. These are not random reflections or ruminations on love; they directly address the divided Corinthian situation and counsel love as its remedy. We see this especially in Paul's final exhortation in the letter (16:14), which sums up his appeal for unity: "Let things be yours in love."

Paul's insistence on the centrality of love for a Christian community seems enduringly, absolutely essential. If the church is not characterized by love, could it possibly be living out its mandate, its call to love God and neighbor? If not for love, what does the church stand for? But where is there room here for a love that uproots, shakes the rafters in the quest for faithfulness, does more than keep the peace? Has love at times been so domesticated by the church that it becomes a code word for passivity or compliance?

The Need to Seek "The Common Advantage"

The root of factionalism, according to Greco-Roman political theory, is the propensity for individuals or subgroups to seek their own advantage or interest instead of the common advantage (that's why we call them "special interest groups"). Therefore the direct response to factionalism is a call to the contenders to put the common advantage over their own individual benefits. Paul employs this argument repeatedly in 1 Corinthians (612; 10:23 —11:1 12:7; 13:5). He urges the Corinthians to compromise voluntarily their right to do things which they can do for the sake of the common good and thus true freedom (esp. ch. 9; 10:23 —11:1; ch. 14). Unity can only be achieved by the compromise of individual advantage for the sake of the common advantage (10:24, 33). The fourth-century church father John Chrysostom called this "the rule of the most perfect Christianity" (Homily 25 on 1 Corinthians): "Seeking not my own advantage, but that of the many, so that they might be saved" (10:33).

Paul's emphasis on the common good over individual goods has great relevance and power for us today, as many think our own American culture is especially destitute in this regard. For instance, it is commonplace election-year strategy among pollsters and spin doctors that voters will decide solely on the basis of the impact (anticipated or actual) of policies on their own pocketbooks. In the church, too, people exhibit a consumer mentality, shopping for the church that will offer them the services they need rather than for a community to join to whose common purpose they wish to contribute. No church can survive unless it is defined by a common advantage for which all work.

On the other hand, who decides and controls "the common advantage"? We know from our own political experience that "the common advantage" can become mere propaganda for "the advantage of those who are in charge" (state socialism has had this charge laid against it, and it has played a key role in current anti-Washington polemical politics). Secondly, what are the limits of individual compromise? Paul describes the absolute extreme of the compromiser when he describes himself as "all things to all people" (9:22) and as "pleasing to all people in every way" (10:33), yet don't we distrust such people? Where is personal integrity in such a strategy? When must one do what doesn't please people for the sake of a larger, as-yet-unaccepted common good? What are the limits of the individual's need to compromise for the sake of the whole? When does "seeking the common advantage" mean "being taken advantage of"? When do such compromises become forms of oppression that must be named and overcome?

Insider and Outsiders

It is commonplace political wisdom that if you want to unify your country, start a war. One strategy for consolidating group loyalty is to stress the distinction between the political body itself and "outsiders," which is precisely what Paul does in 1 Corinthians 5:12 — 6:6 (using exactly this language). His argument to the church is in essence that we must be unified because we are a bastion of truth in a hostile world. Such thinking is the basis of sectarian sociology and was indeed a large part of the social power of the early church — the church vs. the world (a view which reached its apex in Gnostic Christianity). We can see it also in Paul's argument in 1:22 – 24, where Paul delimits the church as a "third race," termed "the called ones," who are separate from Jews and Greeks (see also 10:32). Yet such a perspective can lead to the false assurance that evil is outside the church only and could render a church incapable of recognizing and dealing with its own failures. It also may seek too soon to defuse and "resolve" conflicts as soon as they surface in such a way that the church does not allow itself to be challenged, to change or to grow. Any impetus for change in the church could be rebuffed by the claim to need to guard against the outside world at all costs. The other difficulty with this strategy for modern Christians is that it is becoming less and less compatible with modern pluralistic perspectives and religious (and nonreligious) tolerance and mutual respect. A church unity that is won at the cost of demonizing the rest of the world may result in an isolated and paranoid church, cut off from any sense of place or mission in the larger culture and world. It raises the question: Unity for what?

Maintain the Status Quo

Arguments for unity are inherently conservative in ideology, for they incorporate a "don't rock the boat" mentality. It is often remarked that it is those who are in comfortable positions in the current social order who appeal for unity by maintaining the status quo, for they have the most to gain thereby and the most to lose in reconfigurations of the group. In 1 Corinthians there are three famous (or infamous) texts in which Paul uses such arguments in his quest to preserve group unity and stability: 7:17–24 (slaves should stay as they are); 11:2–16 (women should wear a headcovering in liturgical prayer or prophecy); and 14:33b–36 (women should be silenced in the assembly). This emphasis on retaining the status quo is consonant with Paul's use of the body metaphor, as we have seen, which views the social order as divinely ordained and legitimated, and which does not (cannot) make provision for status alteration. These passages also can be understood in the light of Paul's apocalyptic perspective (7:29, 31; 10:11). When one is sure that the world is about to end, there is no sense in fomenting revolution of the doomed and temporary social order.

What a fascinating paradox this man Paul was! He talked about the end of the world coming soon but also about laying down a firm, enduring foundation for the church! This paradox (to believe that life and history are in God's hands but to live as though they were in ours) is one of the central tensions of modern Christian existence. Modern Christians, who less and less share Paul's apocalyptic view (unless replaced with a non-divine, world-ending intervention) are perhaps less and less patient of such an acceptance of social structures which deprive classes, genders or races of people from full participation in the benefits of life and society. At the same time, this leads us to recognize that efforts to change the social order in the name of justice must also realize and reckon with the fact that one casualty of those efforts may be unity within the church. The burning question remains: When is unity the value to be pursued, and when justice, if we cannot have both? Both are important, but often we must choose. How do we make those choices?

We have examined seven elements of Paul's continuous   **Conclusion**
argument for unity and reconciliation in 1 Corinthians:
appealing to the "ones" which all Christians share, to the church as the body of
Christ, to the church as God's Building/the Temple of the Holy Spirit, to the
need to "seek to common advantage" instead of private advantage, stressing the
distinction between insiders and outsiders to cement group solidarity, and
appealing to the status quo (in the case of slaves and women) not to upset the
applecart. Throughout the examination of these arguments, I have stressed that
each has both positive and negative possibilities for Christian ecclesiology in
practice, for contemporary strategies of reconciliation. The dual legacy of 1
Corinthians, which signals the complexity of the quest for reconciliation itself,
is: (1) First Corinthians is the most eloquent, moving and challenging call to
unity within the church which the tradition has produced, and its place in the
canon rightly assures that it speaks with power to each new Christian generation of that important value of unity; and (2) the urgent call for unity that Paul
makes in 1 Corinthians is not without its cost: Unity must be bought at a price.
At its best, this price may be mutual and just compromise; at its worst, it may
entail conformity, mental or spiritual lockstep, or legitimation of an unjust
social status quo. How shall we choose to embody this legacy?

For Pastoral Reflection and Response

Can it be good news when even Paul's arguments for unity and reconciliation in the church fail? What possible hope can we have in our efforts if a persuasive preacher like Paul cannot convince the church of his time? Dr. Mitchell's presentation is sobering indeed, but not despairing, for Paul is still today urging the church to the ministry and reality of reconciliation every time we read 1 Corinthians. What motivates Paul motivates us: the gospel of reconciliation entrusted to us by Christ and the commission to proclaim it.

How can we pastor like Paul, knowing that every image and strategy of unity we try has its promises and its pitfalls, its possibilities and its limitations? Our primary concern must be for the living faith of those who are believers in Christ, to point out what is at the heart and essence of Christian faith. We strive to help believers understand how to relate to one another out of their relationship with the Spirit of the triune God. This means that any pastoring for the sake of reconciliation has as its touchstone the meaning of baptism. In baptism each believer becomes a member of the body of Christ, the church; each one is a locus of the Spirit's action, uniquely gifted in the Spirit (1 Corinthians 12). In light of this great mystery, can a believer ever truly say, "I don't belong?" Can the church ever say, "You don't belong?" In our pastoral ministry, do we see everyone in the body without exception as "indispensable" (1 Corinthians 12:22)? Do we give the impression by our speech or actions that there are insiders and outsiders, more honorable and less honorable, even within the body?

How do we build up the body of Christ? How can we empower believers for the unity celebrated in baptism and eucharist, for the ministry of reconciliation? Answers to these questions are found by asking another question: Is reconciliation in Christ worth working for, fighting for, dying for? Is it alive in our memory and imagination? If 1 Corinthians found a place in the canon of Christian scriptures, it is because it seduced the memory and imagination with tales of values worth fighting for, worth dying for.

This living (and admittedly dangerous) memory and imagination will ignite in our own time if we trust the instinct of the liturgical renewal in restoring the liturgy of the word to every sacramental and liturgical celebration and process. If we are a body, a building, built up and held together in love, we are so by the word of God. How well are liturgies of the word celebrated? Are the texts well-prepared and delivered? Is the music appropriate? Is there adequate silence for the word to speak to each person's heart? What of the preaching and catechesis that flows from the texts in Sunday eucharist, children's liturgy of the word, catechumenates, reconciling communities and sacramental celebrations? Do they combine concrete circumstance and scriptural wisdom so that the truth of God is revealed in a seductive and compelling way? In particular, all experience of sin, division and reconciliation must be made subject to the biblical word.

To facilitate this dialogue of human circumstance and scripture that enlivens the central core of Christian truth, at least three strategies will help cut the cost of reconciliation.

First, pastoral ministers need to remain in dialogue with critical scholarship. It is scholarship's job to alert us to the behavior of metaphors, to their limits, to their need to flock together for mutual correcting. It is scholarship's job to ferret out pre-understandings which create barriers and boundaries that obscure vision. It is scholarship's task to uncover ideologies — for example, of power, gender, or God — that alienate. The work of scholarship is essential to retrieving stories, enlivening memory and exorcising the demons of mental dullness.

Second, pastoral ministers need to trust people's common sense. There is an innate poetic sense in people that helps them know how the scriptures construct the ways of being in the world. Engendering poets is the purpose of living liturgies of the word; conception takes place through the people's active listening and responding to the storied word. There is growing testimony to this creativity in the working of faith-sharing groups in our churches or in catechumenates, in the experience of small Christian communities, in families who live the metaphor of sitting down to the table of the word, in the individual who actively listens to and meditates on the word of God. While factions are a constant danger in social and ecclesial life, the creative and self-correcting potential of Christian believers, especially in small groups, needs to be encouraged as a cost-cutting safeguard.

Third, pastoral ministers need to recognize and admit their limits in the work of restoring unity, healing or reconciliation, and need to call upon the particular skills necessary to facilitate the unfolding of individual and communal stories, the unpeeling of their many layers. We need to distinguish among the ministries of spiritual direction, spiritual companioning, pastoral counseling and pastoral care. We need to draw wisely upon the support services of mental health professionals, psychotherapy, counseling and various support groups. The ministry of reconciliation cannot depend upon one or a few persons only. The whole community, in the wealth of its gifts and skills, is needed.

Thus all of Paul's arguments are social in nature: the "ones" that unite in diversity, the members of one body, the materials of God's building, the love that holds it all together, and so on. Paul's concern (and it remains with us today) is how the unity of the church will be manifest. This is not a concern only about the internal life of the church but about how the church is in the world. How does the body of Christ build up the body of humankind? How is the church the embassy of reconciliation (see 2 Corinthians 5:17ff) in the world? This is the church's work of justice, which needs to be operative at every level of church life, from the hierarchical magisterium to diocesan and parochial activity and advocacy to the witness of the individual. How do we work to include those who find themselves outsiders because of economics, race or ethnic heritage, physical or mental ability, gender, sexual orientation, level of education, illness, political ideology or any of the innumerable ways we can divide one from another? When are compromise or maintaining the status quo just strategies? When are they unjust? What is "the common advantage" in God's eyes, from the perspective of the Christian gospel?

If we are to answer these questions, if we are to move toward success in the work of reconciliation, we need to tell the Corinthian story — and the Lucan story, and the Johannine story, and all the stories of God's People — over and over and over again. Believers need to listen to them again and again in order to know their truth more deeply and clearly, and so to live that truth more fully. We are still, like the Corinthians, a very young Christian community, but a steady diet of God's Word will help the body grow in health and maturity and will lead us in the ways of love.

The oral responses given at the symposium by Eugene King, OMI, then rector of St. Paul University Seminary, Ottawa, Ontario, Canada, and Donna Steffen, SC, spiritual director and minister of initiation from Cincinnati, Ohio, contributed greatly to these pastoral notes.

History and the Reform of Penance

James Dallen

The church has always given tradition pride of place, especially when engaging in reform and renewal. Vatican Council II was no exception. According to the *Constitution on the Sacred Liturgy,* revision is to be "in the light of sound tradition"[1] and "new forms [should] grow in some way organically out of the forms already existing."[2] The norm was stated clearly: "In order that healthy tradition can be preserved while yet allowing room for legitimate development, thorough investigation — theological, historical, and pastoral — of the individual parts of the liturgy up for revision is always to be the first step."[3]

The committee responsible for drafting the revised penance ritual took the norm seriously. Their first report to the Consilium included a 15-page historical survey representing scholarly consensus on development through the twelfth century.[4] The heavily footnoted overview summarized points from key documents and indicated features of the sacrament in different periods in West and East.[5] It highlighted the communal and ecclesial nature and effect of "ecclesiastical penance" in the ancient period in the West and of Eastern penance in general — the direction of reform called for by the Council[6] — and indicated characteristics and consequences for pastoral practice.[7] The committee then grounded its reform proposals in historical precedent.[8]

The bare-bones overview largely ignored earlier historiographical controversies, especially polemics over the antiquity of private confession.[9] Taking history even more seriously than had the *Constitution on the Sacred Liturgy,* it recognized variety, change and development — a major step forward.[10] Less positively, it failed to situate the evolving forms in relation to one another and in relation to their socio-cultural and pastoral contexts.

Such analysis is necessary in order to understand how the varying forms of penance functioned in the religious life of communities and individuals, and why they took their characteristic shapes. Attempts have been made to account for development as well as describe it,[11] but that kind of history of penance largely remains to be written. Popular religion — how ordinary people believed, worshiped and lived — is only beginning to be investigated, and the scarcity of sources makes any reconstruction speculative and tentative. With earlier historiographical controversies between Catholics and Protestants, and Jansenists and Modernists, transcended, there is now a basic consensus on the general lines of development in the history of penance.[12] The most significant consensus, well established before Vatican Council II, concerns ancient penance: It was communal and ecclesial in character and purpose, intended to restore the penitent sinner to an active role among the faithful—symbolized by full eucharistic participation—and to restore the church to wholeness.[13]

Theologians have taken advantage of historical research as a foundation for reform proposals, and it is that dimension of the history of penance that I wish to examine, looking at the ancient, medieval and modern periods. In each case I will note characteristic features of penance in that period. In a concluding section I will comment on aspects likely to be useful for ongoing reform.

What I want to emphasize at the outset is that the varied forms of penance throughout most of its history do not fit into well-defined categories. In particular, the use of two sets of dichotomous categories needs to be suspended: public or private penance, nonsacramental or sacramental penance. Both sets of categories have been prominent in polemics and controversies regarding penance, and both have been used anachronistically. The dichotomy between public and private penance is useless and misleading prior to the Carolingian era. The dichotomy between sacramental and nonsacramental penance is an artificial thirteenth-century scholastic construct that played no part in religious life in preceding centuries and whose practical pastoral value is questionable today, especially since it is now more canonical than theological.

A final preliminary comment regarding liturgical ritual and Christian reality: Achieving the goal of penance reform is not to be gauged by the frequency of sacramental celebration. "Liturgy is not the only activity of the church,"[14] even if it is "the high point towards which the activity of the church is directed, and, simultaneously, the source from which all its power flows out."[15] The task is to continue and strengthen the rhythms of conversion established in baptism and maintained by eucharist—to call Christian people to continued conversion and to support them in that, not to get them to go to confession more often. Historical reflection may lead to the conclusion that the sacrament should always be available to all rather than merely to a few—a product of the historical development—but it also shows the risks involved in insisting on it for all sinners or in a particular form. It also shows that ritual must not substitute for reality.

With these cautions in mind, let us look at the history of penance, beginning with the origins of ancient penance.

Ancient Penance

The institution of the sacraments has come to be looked at very differently since the middle of the twentieth century. Bernard Leeming, for example, while limiting the *substantia* of a sacrament to its meaning, held for an immediate institution of the sacraments by Christ.[16] The *Catechism of the Catholic Church* approaches the modernist understanding of mediate institution condemned by Pius X[17] when it regards the mysteries of Christ's life as the foundation of the actions of the Spirit at work in his body, the church.[18]

Yet this comes closer to what we can discern of the historical origins of the sacrament of penance and reconciliation, as we now call it. It appears to have emerged, amid controversy, as an expression of the church's authority to deal as decisively with its members' sin after baptism as it did when baptizing them. It emerged as part of the church's service to God, humanity and its members in order to maintain the church as a clear sacramental sign of God's salvation. In its origins, then, penance had a strong soteriological and eschatological thrust in relation to the church's mission.

The critical and controversial issue was how to deal with the "faithful" who had abandoned their baptismal commitment, and this is the element of penance that has received the most attention. Practice and policy varied by time and place, but it was generally accepted in the ancient church that the good of both the church and penitent sinners required segregation and intensive ministry for those whose way of life sharply contradicted that of the Christian community. The church showed its responsibility to guide and critique the conversion of others, everyday sinners, by calling them to continued conversion and supporting that conversion. It did this by example, by loving concern and by prayer, ritualizing these primarily in the eucharistic celebration.

Amid continuing controversy, a penitential institution paralleling the catechumenate was established for those whose fall into serious sin showed that the dynamic of conversion had ceased to govern their lives. This institution, the order of penitents, was perhaps first established in northern Africa at the beginning of the third century.[19] The operative pastoral premises in the parallel institutions supporting first and second conversion were that orienting and reorienting people to continued conversion takes time and requires the community's assistance. In both transitional institutions, there was an initial ritual marking individuals' new status as members of a distinct group within the church, a special community ministry during their membership in the group, and a concluding ritual at the end of which they took their places at the eucharistic table with the faithful.[20] Their communion with the faithful in celebrating the eucharist was the clearest sign that their transitional status had ceased, though former penitents — like convicted felons today — often had lifelong restrictions placed on them. The most striking was that they were henceforth ineligible to enter penance and be reconciled.[21]

These continuing penalties show that the Western attitude toward repentant sinners was somewhat grudging and punitive, the consequence of controversies over reconciliation. People had entered penance voluntarily, even when "encouraged," but eventually canons insisted on sinners submitting to the discipline. In line with the Roman emphasis on law and order and the need to balance off wrongdoing, the institutional structures required external signs of conversion to test the depth and sincerity of repentance before granting reconciliation. The same Spirit on which everyday sinners depended inspired conversion and showed its presence in prayer, fasting, almsgiving and other works of penance, even in those who had become "faithless." Still, even after reconciliation, former penitents remained somewhat suspect.

Another perspective on this history, however, focuses on the fact that most Christians were forbidden to enter formal penance and continued or resumed conversion informally. It suggests that perhaps the ancient outlook regarded the average person who had sinned as capable of repenting and resuming the ongoing conversion of baptismal life without the intensive community care provided in the order of penitents. As responsible adults, they were able to look for and find the help they needed. From this perspective, the exclusion of so many people from formal penance is more expressive of pastoral common sense than it is of vindictiveness.[22]

Ancient penance has caught the attention of historians, theologians and reformers because the communal process of the order of penitents contrasts so sharply with the highly individualized ritual of recent centuries. However, the mediating role of the church was also part of the consciousness of ordinary sinners. The order of penitents, impressive though it may seem to us, had hardly any part in the religious life of the vast majority of Christians during the period. They too found community support for their ongoing conversion but in less intensive and more ordinary forms. Cultural factors fixed attention on bodily behavior rather than introspective feelings, so self-denial, while reaching out to God in prayer and to neighbor in service, was the solution to everyday sin. Church support was experienced through other Christians' example, loving concern and prayer, with the eucharist having a privileged place.

In the East, spiritual directors and monks, as well as clerics, often provided a ministry for sinners not eligible for entrance into the order of penitents, especially for monks but also for laity. (This appears to have been the only specialized ministry apart from those for members of the order of penitents.) In the East as early as the third century, the manifestation of conscience to a spiritual director was an alternate way of beginning penance, though not a substitute for the official procedures. Presbyters in sixth- and seventh-century Gaul who were offering spiritual direction both to everyday sinners and to penitents preparing for episcopal reconciliation had a ministry closely related to that being developed by Anglo-Saxon and Irish monk-confessors on the Eastern model.

The transitional state as a penitent was short for those who were dying: They were given penance and immediately reconciled. This emergency adaptation of canonical penance — the only private form of official penance ministry in the ancient period — became common and popular, and in some places was not only encouraged but required, even for clerics. This form of ecclesiastical penance shows that the official institution was motivated by pastoral compassion and flexible enough to adapt; but its growth in frequency and popularity is a sign that penance and conversion were coming to be understood as something that could be given ritually when it was not possible to live it.

Canonically regulated in the fourth and fifth centuries to the point of exhaustion, the order of penitents ceased to be a significant institution in the sixth and seventh centuries. However, canonically regulated penance took forms other than the order of penitents even when that institution was still vigorous.

Some of these forms outlived the order of penitents and lasted well into the Middle Ages. The order of penitents mutated into a group known as the *conversi,* converging with monasticism.[23] Pious layfolk dedicated themselves to a more religious way of life, sometimes remaining in their communities, sometimes becoming associated with monasteries. Closely related to the *conversi,* though adopting a penitential way of life only temporarily, were those who went on pilgrimage. This too became even more important during the Middle Ages.

The earliest form of repeatable penance is another outgrowth of the canonical order of penitents: lenten penance. After the demise of the catechumenate and the deterioration of the order of penitents, the character of Lent shifted from baptismal to penitential, and the community began to follow the penitents rather than lead the catechumens. As early as the beginning of the fifth century, people became ceremonial penitents for Lent.

Penance took a variety of forms in the ancient period, all of which were intended to restore or maintain the baptismal rhythms of conversion in people's lives. Historians and theologians have focused on the extraordinary and intense ministry offered those Christians whose fall into serious sin showed that they had ceased to undergo conversion. This ministry was focused on reorienting them to conversion and thus restoring the church to wholeness so that it could accomplish its mission as a sign of salvation. Penitents were freed from sin because they had completed the process of resuming conversion — the Latin *absolutio* meant not only acquittal but also completion and was the church's blessing on those who had now returned to the path of conversion. The context was a community whose members were challenged and supported to live lives of conversion.

To use later scholastic terms for the situation in the ancient church, the "sacrament" of penance or conversion was rare, but the "virtue" of penance was common. That may be an overly idealized picture, but it does keep our attention fixed on the foundational context for extraordinary ministries. Ministry to serious sinners, rare and extraordinary though it may have been, had as its goal helping them to take their places in a converting community. We need to look more closely at how the call to conversion was maintained in the lives of everyday sinners and to broaden our notion of sacramentality to include these means as well.

Medieval Penance

Focus shifted in the Middle Ages from the conversion and reconciliation of the faith ful to the forgiveness of sins. Distinctions came to be made between private and public forgiveness and between sacramental and nonsacramental means of forgiveness. Narrowing of vision was compensated for by a broadened availability of ministries and rituals that had formerly been extraordinary. Old forms died and new ones arose.

Nevertheless, outgrowths of canonical penance survived well into the Middle Ages. The order of penitents continued as *paenitentia solemnis,* though it was rarely used. The *conversi* continued as an identifiable group, giving rise to several penitential movements. A segment of this penitential movement became "regularized" in the thirteenth century when Francis of Assisi became a *conversus* and later established rules of life for orders of penance for vowed men, vowed women and lay people.[24] Pilgrimage remained a popular way to expiate sin. Like the penitential practices of the *conversi* and the official penitents, pilgrimage, including the Crusades, was an external sign of repentance and rededication.[25] Lenten penance was an annual challenge and opportunity for doing penance, and by the tenth century, all Christians were expected to observe it. A new element was also introduced that eventually would lead to our modern private confession.

Earlier heated controversies have cooled, and it is now generally agreed that no "private" penance existed during the ancient period that was a practical alternative to the "public" procedures of the order of penitents. However, Anglo-Saxon and Celtic monks had begun to extend to the laity the "informal" penance, spiritual direction and counseling that they had borrowed from Eastern monasticism. Unlike canonical penance, this informal and unofficial practice did not segregate sinners into an identifiable group, offered no ministry in public liturgy and provided no ritual of reconciliation. In addition, it was always available for all converting sinners — this, I believe, is more significant than that it was repeatable.

The monastic practice underwent significant change as it was extended to laity barely evangelized. What had begun as a manifestation of conscience for the sake of spiritual guidance on continuing conversion and spiritual growth came to have a ritual value in its own right: a confession of sins so that the confessor could advise on appropriate means of making satisfaction for these sins. The work of Irish missionaries on the continent in the sixth and seventh centuries established the practice there, and it quickly became popular. So far as demands put on the penitent were concerned, it appeared much the same as canonical penance, but it was private, without subsequent consequences and repeatable. What it lacked was a ritual officially reconciling the sinner with the church. This, I believe, correlates with an individualistic and introspective penitential piety that undermined reform efforts then and undermines them now.[26] Because it contravened the canons and bypassed the bishop, the tariff system was repeatedly condemned by Carolingian reform councils, and efforts were made to ban the penitentials, books which monk-confessors used to determine how much penance a given sin was worth.

Some bishops and councils tolerated the practice for sins that were not subject to canonical discipline. A more far-reaching compromise allowed private penance for grave sins that were not publicly known: The penitent was to confess to a priest and then return for reconciliation after completing the assigned penance — the procedures of canonical penance done privately under the priest's supervision. The difficulty of getting penitents accustomed to the Irish practice to return for reconciliation led by the mid-tenth century to an immediate reconciliation following the confession and assignment of penance. Lay and monastic confession, without official reconciliation, continued into the fourteenth century, however.[27]

Neither the Carolingian compromise nor the immediate joining of a ritual of reconciliation to confession was yet our private confession. Before that could evolve, confession of sins had to take on the role previously played by satisfaction, absolution had to have a causal role in the forgiveness of sins, and canonical regulation had to give this ritual primary place in the forgiveness of postbaptismal sins. By the end of the twelfth century, oral confession had come to be regarded as the essential means of expiating sin, and an indicative formula of absolution was commonly used — confession and absolution had replaced confession and satisfaction as the central factor in obtaining divine forgiveness. Lateran Council IV (1215), obliging all who had reached the age of discretion to make an annual confession to their priest, began the official transition to modern penance.

The emphasis that came to be given to absolution is evidence of converging shifts in perspective. In baptism, penance and spirituality in general, sin and its forgiveness became a matter of preoccupation. Other elements of Christian transformation receded into the background: union with Christ, incorporation into the church, reception of the Spirit, new life. Individual effort was needed to escape the consequences of sin by making satisfaction for it. Authoritative rituals consoled and reassured the insecure that their sins were forgiven. Through confession individuals purged themselves of guilt, and through absolution they received forgiveness.

One other new form of penance developed in the Middle Ages: general absolutions. These declarations of the forgiveness of sins began to be used in the Liturgy of the Hours and in the Mass in the ninth century and remained popular until the late Middle Ages, especially during Lent and on communion days. Their relevance for the contemporary issue of so-called "general" absolution is often noted.[28]

Scholastic theologians developed the concept of sacramentality in a manner that excluded general absolutions, lay confession and the remnants of ancient canonical penance, *paenitentia solemnis,* pilgrimage, the penitential movements and lenten penance. These were of value only in forgiving venial sins. The process was soon complete: By the fifteenth century only private confession survived as an officially recognized means of forgiveness for sins committed after baptism. For many people, including the influential Scotus, absolution was the heart of the sacrament, for it was the official guarantee of forgiveness. In both baptism and penance, conversion was not so much something to be experienced in everyday terms as something to be received ritually.

Modern Penance

Further sixteenth-century developments gave modern penance its characteristic features. Responding to the Protestant reformers' rejection of individual auricular confession and priestly absolution, the Council of Trent responded as had the bishops of the Carolingian era by eliminating abuses, reaffirming the official procedures and encouraging or requiring their use. Procedures were paramount: confession to the priest and absolution by the priest. Though private and individual, these procedures functioned as significant expressions of adherence to the church community.

The reformed 1614 ritual of Paul V accents the priest's role as judge, and its "liturgy" is quick, efficient and almost nonliturgical. Scholastic theology's preoccupation with confession and absolution showed itself in a minimizing of elements of praise and prayer, the elimination of social and ecclesial references and the exclusion of the penitent from an active liturgical role. With the growing frequency of confession in the era of the Counter-Reformation and with an even greater emphasis on confession and absolution in opposition to Protestant objections, even the little prayer by priest and penitent that remained was eventually lost. As the vernacular was introduced in the 1960s, priests reduced their part in the "liturgy" to the essential words of absolution and encouraged penitents to pray the act of contrition before entering the confessional.

Nonsacramental means of forgiveness continued to be mentioned and used throughout the era of the Counter-Reformation. Nevertheless, the sacrament that came to be termed "confession" was the most significant means of forgiveness. Outside the sacrament, forgiveness was possible only through "perfect" contrition. In the sacrament, "imperfect" contrition was sufficient; the church's ritual of absolution compensated for what was lacking in the individual person.

Lessons from History?

What can we learn from this history to help us in the work of ongoing reform and renewal? I would first emphasize something that we have learned about theological and liturgical history. We have learned that history is the story of change and that it goes beyond mere incidentals. Few areas of worship have changed as radically over the centuries as has the sacrament of penance and reconciliation. No one today, for example, is likely to think that St. Joseph built the first confessional according to blueprints drawn by Jesus or that private auricular confession has always existed. We also have transcended the nineteenth-century myth of progress. Only a small minority today would want to claim that the centuries conspired together to give us the gift of private confession as we have known it.[29] Since the emergence of scientific history and the rise of historical consciousness, we have come to acknowledge, accept and even celebrate the reality of change in the church, always in a cultural context, generally for pastoral reasons, sometimes for the better.

What is most heartening in this history is the variety and flexibility the sacrament has shown. Local churches have generally found ways in their differing situations to respond pastorally to current needs, usually in multiple ways. Only in the modern period has the church been content with one all-purpose form of the sacrament. For much of this history, the focus and context of the ministry officially offered to sinners was a community undergoing conversion. But as the sense of community and ongoing conversion changed and weakened, the rituals for authenticating and celebrating conversion became ends in themselves.

Most who have written on lessons to be learned from history have confined themselves to the ancient period and stressed that the sacrament is social and ecclesial in character, ministry and outcome.[30] This element, largely lost for centuries, was the primary motivation for Vatican II's reform, Pope John Paul II to the contrary,[31] and it certainly needs to become part of our experience again. Efforts to restore this social and ecclesial dimension to consciousness have taken various forms and have had varying degrees of success: revitalizing the virtue of penance and penitential practices, provision for communal celebrations of the sacrament, a communal penitential rite in the Mass, a new order of penitents.

Much of the official ambivalence regarding communal celebrations has centered on the fully communal celebration, in which both the confession and the proclamation of reconciliation take place publicly and communally.[32] The ambivalence, I believe, is largely due to familiarity in recent centuries with only individual confession and a tendency to see the individual and communal forms as competitive rather than complementary. Historical perspective may be helpful, as community forms and ministries have been dominant throughout most of the history without detriment to the personal dimension.

We might benefit from a shift of perspective. Since the resolution of the third-century penitential controversies, it has been customary to focus almost exclusively on the conclusion of the process, the rite of reconciliation. That we still do so is evident not only in the cumbersome name we now give the sacrament but also in the controversies over the communal proclamation of reconciliation and the devaluing of the "nonsacramental" penitential celebrations because they lack a definitive absolution.

It would be helpful to focus instead on the process itself, the process of conversion. "Reconciliation" applies properly only to the empowering force and ultimate goal of a life of conversion — the action of God in Christ reaching us through the Spirit — and in the extreme cases where individuals have ceased conversion and seek to resume it. In other words, individuals are not reconciled to the church if they have not been separated from it by serious sin, but they do feel the reconciling love of God in Christ sustaining them as they continue to be transformed by the Spirit into the likeness of Christ. The reformed ritual, the *Rite of Penance,* itself suggests this broader perspective, as "penance" means "conversion."

Recognizing this helps us see the value of the sacrament for living the Christian life, even when people are not conscious of serious sin. It also makes it easier to recognize the variety of ways in which we call one another to continue or resume conversion and support one another in doing so. "The whole church, as a priestly people, acts in different ways in the work of reconciliation which has been entrusted to it by the Lord."[33] Yes, that statement is made in the *Rite of Penance,* but the *Rite* in fact deals directly only with that ministry as it is exercised by presbyters and bishops. Other forms of ministry also need to be recognized.

We know almost nothing of the variety of ministries that must have existed for the ancient order of penitents, although they probably paralleled the ministries that existed for catechumens. We know more of means available in the Middle Ages in addition to those directly expressive of the power of the keys restoring individuals to full communion with the faithful, but further study of these "nonsacramental" forms is still needed. Implementing the conciliar reforms requires looking beyond the forgiveness of individuals' sins to the broader reality of reconciliation. It also requires recognizing that ecclesial reconciliation presumes and depends upon conversion, even as conversion itself presumes and depends upon God in Christ reconciling the world to God's own self.

Our challenge is not so much to imagine new forms for reconciling sinners as it is to creatively call one another to deeper conversion. Such conversion is a process — not a program, not a ritual. It is a process intimately personal and deeply communal.

First we must live with our sinfulness until we intimately know its evil, realize that it is out of our control and make the decision to surrender ourselves to God. That is contrition, a turning from sin and a turning to God whereby we begin or renew our conversion. At this stage we may not even be able to name our sinfulness or recognize its characteristic features, but we see in Christ what we yearn to be.

Then we must look at our lives closely to see where we have gone astray, admit to ourselves, to God and to at least one other human being "the exact nature of our wrongs,"[34] be ready to change and ask God to change us. That is confession. In the course of history, confession's manner and minister has varied, but experience has shown that sin must be named and our consciousness of sin must be shared in some way with at least one companion if we are to proceed on the path of conversion.

We must identify those whom we have harmed, be willing to make amends, and do so to the extent possible. That is satisfaction. Life must be restructured, relationships must be rebuilt, the evil that has been done must be undone, or conversion is no more than a wistful dream.

But something more is still needed if absolution is to have full meaning as the *absolutio* or completion of conversion. We must continue to commit to the path of conversion. We must reach out to God in prayer and to others in sharing "the message of reconciliation"[35] as "ambassadors of Christ."[36] Individually and together, we must be on mission. That is the element that has been least appreciated in recent centuries — unity for the sake of mission.

You perhaps recognize in the description I have given not only the traditional "acts of the penitent" but the Twelve Steps of Alcoholics Anonymous, which has rediscovered the communal process of penance and conversion developed in the early church. Like any addiction, sin has its claws in us and drags us around, toying with us as a cat with a mouse. Alone, we are lost. Together, we can move forward. In the church, we can experience even now Christ's victory over sin and death that God will share with us when the cosmos reaches its goal.

The personal and ecclesial dimensions of conversion are still not well integrated ritually or theologically, and rituals that accent either the personal or the communal are often set against one another. Yet none of those rituals really focus directly on conversion. The rite for reconciling individuals gives individuals the opportunity to reflect upon their experience of conversion in an atmosphere of shared prayer, but in practice this is reduced to listing sins, and the role of the minister is to declare reconciliation — or more accurately, to bless the penitent's conversion in the name of the church and to share the Spirit that sustains conversion. The rites for reconciling groups of penitents show that community is the context of reconciliation, but the role and ministry of the community is little developed beyond the common admission of sinfulness. The call to conversion is clearer and more sustained, but the outcome of conversion, the church's blessing on it and the proclamation of reconciliation, is still the primary focus, as shown in the controversies over whether it is to be communal or individual. Only the "nonsacramental" penitential celebrations in the *Rite of Penance* give primary emphasis to the process of conversion itself, but they are even more neglected than are the sacramental forms.

The new order of penitents also gives attention to restoring the sense of conversion to people's lives.[37] It brings out that conversion is a process that needs to be fostered and sustained throughout.[38] Modeled as it is on the *Rite of Christian Initiation of Adults* and twelve-step programs, it offers greater opportunity for the development of a variety of ministries in and of the community. It has been an effective means of providing "conversion therapy" for Catholics returning to the church because it does not move too quickly to reconciliation. Yet necessary as this ministry is, as such it can touch only a small part of the church. Something like it, especially during Lent, is needed for a greater number of people in our parishes.

Over the course of history the ritual proclamation of reconciliation has come to be available to all sinners at all times. At the same time, the need to sustain conversion in other ways and through other community ministries has received less attention. This is happening, to be sure, and probably in a broader and more solidly founded way than has been true for centuries. Faith-sharing and spiritual direction, for example, are no longer limited to the spiritual elite, and participation in such ministries is not limited to clergy. Still, we too rarely see these "nonsacramental" means in clear relationship to the sacrament. The study of history shows the need to support all the faithful in responding to the continual call to be transformed into Christ. No single means or ministry, whether labeled sacramental or not, can fill that need. A unifying vision may help us to recognize new signs of hope even as a once-familiar form becomes marginal.

Historically, the forms and ministries of conversion and reconciliation have had a clear relationship to the church's mission as it was envisioned and lived at different periods. Sometimes it has been a matter of maintaining the church as a clear sign of holiness in a pagan society. At other times the church has been more concerned with assisting individuals in saving their souls. In our day, there is a new sense that the church's mission must be more broadly social and extended beyond its boundaries, and the *Rite of Penance* is the first ritual to link sacramental liturgy with work for justice and peace.[39] As we have come to realize again that all the faithful share responsibility for mission, so we must see as well that sacramental reform and renewal are largely fruitless if they do not move us to the service of God and neighbor as participants in the church's mission.[40] That mission is still concerned with resisting evil and exercising Christ's authority over it, whether that evil be in individuals' lives or in society.

Transformation, transcending self in order to enter into deeper relationship with God and neighbor, is the perennial pattern of conversion, whether it be expressed in the ancient triad of prayer, fasting and almsgiving or in a new order of penitents. But all forms, whether old or new, will be credible and effective only to the extent that the church itself is a converting and reconciling community. In those forms, individual or communal, the church is renewed.[41] Bringing that about is the task to which we set ourselves, and success will come only at the end of history.

> All this is from God, who has reconciled us to himself through Christ, and has given us the ministry of reconciliation; that is, in Christ God was reconciling the world to himself, not counting their trespasses against them, and entrusting the message of reconciliation to us. So we are ambassadors for Christ, since God is making his appeal through us; we entreat you on behalf of Christ, be reconciled to God.[42]

For Pastoral Reflection and Response

History is that wise teacher who invites us to look and look again at our past experience and to keep learning from it. Our heritage is too rich and too complex to be told or understood in only one way. We need to approach it from every angle we can in order to mine its riches and truly know what it has to teach us.

Dr. Dallen invites us to look at the history of penance with pastoral eyes. More important than the many forms penance has taken over the ages, he asserts, or the theological interpretations they have been given, is the process of post-baptismal conversion in Christian believers that is at the heart of the rites and theology. And the measure of any reforms of penance is not the frequency of sacramental celebration but how well the church has called people to conversion and supported them in it.

Conversion is the "business" of the church, whether in initiation, reconciliation or the day-to-day nurture of the faithful. Our "mission statement" is to proclaim and mediate the reconciliation we have with God in Christ (see 2 Corinthians 5:18 – 20), resisting sin and evil in the power of the Holy Spirit. Over twenty centuries, the church has adopted many strategies with which to fulfill its mission: rituals of penance and reconciliation, devotional practices, legal sanctions, preaching and catechetical movements. At the core of these strategies has been the pastoral concern to shape and reshape the lives of Christian believers more fully into the life of Christ, a concern that remains with us today.

How will we proceed to fulfill our mission now, based on what we know from our past? A first step in our progress is to name what we do know from the tradition of penance. Here are a few things:

> Despite some early hopes to the contrary, living life in Christ is neither easy nor perfect. Conversion is not a one-time-only turning to the gospel but an ongoing process. Thus the goal of the church's pastoral care is to help believers resume the process of conversion and take their places more fully and knowingly at the eucharistic table.

> The term "penance" is better understood not as isolated actions or occasional signs of good will but as the process that renews baptismal commitment and lifestyle when it has weakened or broken. Reconciliation is properly only for those separated from God and

church by serious sin; penance is for all as they continue their conversion in Christ.

Eucharist is the goal of penance. It encourages and supports ongoing conversion in Christ; its thanksgiving and praise are the proper expression of the penitential process; and it models the mission of inclusivity, reconciliation and unity as we "go forth to love and serve the Lord."

There is a social and communal nature of penance "in character, ministry and outcome." Just as our sin (or any lack of Christian resolve) weakens the body of Christ, so too our renewal of Christian commitment strengthens the body (see *Rite of Penance,* 5). The church's wisdom, resources, pastoral care and skills are available to its members and to the world as they seek to know and love God more deeply and live the gospel life into which they have been incorporated.

The church is *simul justus et peccator,* at the same time a reconciling and converting community. The church needs to be courageous in proclaiming the truth it has received from Christ but humble in acknowledging that this truth is carried in earthenware vessels.

The storehouse of liturgical and devotional practices of penance that have built up over the centuries indicates that communal forms of penance and reconciliation and individual confession are complementary, and not competitive, in the pastoral care of conversion. In addition, the development of the variety of penitential practices until at least the fifteenth century strongly suggests the need for a variety of practices today.

The purpose of penitential and reconciling rituals was — and is — to bless conversion in the name of the church and to share the Holy Spirit who sustains it.

How do these things we have learned from our past help us to meet the present challenge of calling one another creatively to deepen conversion? What are our present practices, and how do they support or obstruct conversion?

If penance and reconciliation are more than rituals, what are the supportive processes for conversion? *The Rite of Penance* (4) suggests Bible study, prayer groups, spiritual direction and faith-sharing groups, and works of mercy and justice as traditional means to this end. But in our own time there is also pastoral counseling, psychotherapy and 12-step support groups, and participation in a variety of groups advocating social justice and peace. There are the formal and informal ways people have for building bridges and making peace in their households, neighborhoods and workplaces. How does this range of church and non-church experiences of healing, forgiveness and liberation come full circle and find expression and depth in the liturgies of the church?

If eucharist is the goal of penance, how does our Sunday gathering and praying, preaching and singing, keeping silence and going forth, deepen post-baptismal conversion in parishioners, parish and church? How does catechesis shape and draw out these kinds of celebrations? How concretely do the ministries of pastoral care in the parish and diocese lead to the Sunday eucharist and empower people for their mission in the world?

If penance is about the renewal and deepening of baptismal commitment in life, how do we restore the place of Lent and the Triduum as the annual, communal time of penance and renewal of baptismal promises? This retreat time, taken with the catechumens, is the opportunity for us to renew and strengthen our perspective: We are on the journey of faith together, constantly learning and relearning life in Christ. How is the Lent/Easter season "programmed" liturgically, catechetically and in service to emphasize the perspective of conversion?

In addition to our usual conduct of "business," however, we need also to ask some questions that may move us beyond "business as usual."

Do we need new rites of penance and reconciliation more suitable to our times? The immediate answer seems to be "yes." The 1973 *Rite of Penance* has not caught on; the mindset, language and needs of our times are not adequately expressed in the liturgical texts; and the use of the three rites of reconciliation seems to be too restricted. Yet it can also be argued that the current rite has barely been explored for its pastoral potential: the rich pastoral theology of its praenotanda, the full liturgical expression of the three rites, the possibilities of additional rituals suggested by paragraphs 36-37, the lectionary of more than 100 scriptural texts. It is true that the full implementation of this rite has been obstructed by old presuppositions about juridical and devotional penance and by a pastoral fear of "cheap grace" replacing pastoral care for conversion. Still, these are not limitations of the rite; they are in us and can be overcome.

The fact remains, nevertheless, that the variety of past penitential practices encourages us to meet the needs of people today with appropriate penitential practices. What rites and processes will adequately heal the wounds of abuse or addiction? How will groups within the parish, diocese or church, divided over issues of clergy conduct, pastoral decisions or style, ecclesial policy or teaching, find a way to mutual dialogue and reconciliation? How will the Christian churches be credible signs of reconciliation in the world if we cannot find a way to be reconciled with one another at the eucharistic table as well as at the baptismal font?

One particular contemporary pastoral concern is outreach to inactive and estranged Catholics. Programs of evangelization and invitation (e.g., the Paulists' "Take Another Look"), a restoration of an order of penitents (e.g., "ReMembering Church," based on the process of Christian initiation; see footnote 37), and other strategies are being developed to minister with these brothers and sisters. A restored order of penitents will have to attend carefully to the problems and pitfalls that led to the demise of similar practices in an earlier period in our history (e.g., its rigorism and its confusion of religious and civic concerns). Any of these strategies will have to recognize that each has its own inherent limitations as well as possibilities, and in any event, they address only a small group of those who are on the road of conversion.

Another question concerns the cultural adaptation of the rites and processes of reconciliation. What is the meaning of conversion, penance and reconciliation among the various cultures and peoples: those from the Pacific rim, those of Hispanic/Latino heritage, those who are deaf and hard of hearing, and so on? Do women forgive and reconcile differently than men, and if so, do we respect that and learn from it? How can we adapt the rites to the genius of the various peoples? What is the content of the mission of reconciliation for the various peoples (e.g., is it different for African Americans than for European Americans)?

Ultimately, when we talk about conversion, we talk about change. But change is a long, difficult and often unwelcome process, needing ever clearer focus and deep commitment. Perhaps, then, the deepest questions for us from our history may be: What is our vision as parish and church of our reconciling mission? Where are we headed, and who is shaping the journey? Are we willing to commit the energy and time it takes to make the vision a reality?

The oral responses given at the symposium by Robert H. Blondell, pastor of St. Isidore Church in Macomb, Michigan, and Jorge Perales, a priest of the Archdiocese of Miami, Florida, greatly contributed to these pastoral notes.

Walking on the Edge of Two Great Abysses Theological Perspectives on Reconciliation

H. Kathleen Hughes, RSCJ

Shortly after the *Rite of Penance* was promulgated, Pope Paul VI addressed the need to reform our way of thinking and also our religious practice relative to the sacrament of reconciliation. He spoke the following words at a general audience in April 1974:

> We are talking precisely about the supreme interest of our life, our own salvation. We are dealing with walking on the edge of two great abysses. . . . The one is that of sin; today's mentality is blinding itself to the existence of sin and blocking out the dizzying sight of sin's lethal and fearsome depths. The other abyss is that of love, of goodness, of mercy, of grace, of resurrection: It is what God offers to our freedom at the level of redemption and of the sacramental activity of the church.[1]

Poised on the edge of two great abysses! Poised between sin and grace, between death and resurrection — not a bad "social location" as we begin a conversation on reconciliation from a theological perspective. And perhaps the only thing more fearsome than being poised at the edge of two great abysses is being ignorant about how precarious our situation actually is and what makes it so, being ignorant about where our feet are planted and what consequences even our slightest movements might have.

It strikes me too that inevitably, as one stands at the edge of these two great abysses, one's attention is captivated by one or the other — by sin or grace, by death or resurrection, by our actions or God's — and that makes all the difference in the judgments we make about the theology and pastoral practice of this rite.

The reflections that follow are organized according to the arrangement of topics in the *praenotanda* to the *Rite of Penance*. Despite the inevitable difficulties and compromises entailed in its preparation, the introduction to a rite remains a critical lens through which one views its theological vision and values. After a few remarks about the preparation of the *Rite of Penance*, I will then explore the various sections in the praenotanda: (1) the mystery of reconciliation in the history of salvation; (2) reconciliation in the church's life; (3) the ministry and many ministers of reconciliation; (4) aspects of the sacramental celebration of reconciliation; and finally, (5) the adaptation of the rite as a theological issue. In the course of this reexamination of the introduction, I will summarize some issues, questions and challenges invited by our experience of the last 20 years.

Preparation of the Revised Rite

The *Constitution on the Sacred Liturgy* gives only the most laconic attention to penance. It states: "The rite and formularies for the sacrament of penance are to be revised so that they more clearly express both the nature and effect of the sacrament."[2] The shortest reform mandate in the liturgy constitution then traveled "a rather long and tortuous road," to quote Archbishop Annibale Bugnini, Secretary of the Consilium overseeing the reform.[3] The reform took ten years, making penance the last major rite to be revised; with it, our new liturgical library was virtually complete.[4]

Bugnini's history of the development of the rite is both interesting and instructive. Questionnaires were sent out; scholarly writings were assembled; conciliar documents were explored. In light of all of these, a number of basic theological theses were formulated to guide the work, chiefly: (1) Sin is by its nature both an offense against God and a wound inflicted on the church; (2) sacramental reconciliation is reconciliation with both God and the church; (3) the entire Christian community works together for the conversion of sinners.[5] In contrast to much earlier theology and practice of sacramental confession, these principles all presume that sin and reconciliation are relational.

Reaching consensus on guiding principles was only preliminary: It is much easier to agree on more abstract theological theses than it is to agree on concrete ritual decisions that give tangible expression to one's theology. Strong differences of opinion surfaced among consultants and among the several dicasteries whose opinions were solicited. For example: Should a declarative form ("I absolve you") or a more ancient deprecative formula of absolution be used — the former emphasizing the role of the minister, the latter the action of God and Christ? Should we have a variety of sacramental formulae that respond to a variety of cases and needs as well as to cultural and regional differences, or are a plurality of formulas a threat to unity and a source of confusion for the faithful? Could penance be celebrated in communal form with general absolution but without prior individual confession, or would this be a possibility only by concession under existing legislation? What is the nature of the sacrament itself, penance or reconciliation, and how should these emphases be balanced? Does one need to include the Tridentine teaching on integral confession, and if so, how could it be incorporated without closing the door to further theological reflection? Should there be any juridical restriction regarding who might ordinarily administer the sacrament or where the sacrament might take place?[6]

In addition, there were strongly expressed reservations about the possibility of including any penitential celebrations at all, even in the appendix to the *Rite of Penance*, since some points were judged "theologically debatable and unacceptable."[7] In the process of the development of the *Rite of Penance*, and given the environment of its final formulation, the basic theological theses about sin, reconciliation and the role of the community were buried in a welter of conflicting concerns and expectations. To that extent the focus on the relational character of sin and reconciliation was also blurred.

Further complicating an assessment of reconciliation is that its implementation has coincided with two decades of profound changes in our church and world. To cite only a few examples: With the break-up of the Soviet Union, we have witnessed the decline of a bipolar world order whose power vacuum has not yet been filled but which has unleashed ancient ethnic and racial animosities. The development of feminist consciousness has challenged our self-understanding, our God images and the way we relate to one another in the body of Christ. Recognition of the multicultural face of our communities, not to mention our growing global consciousness, demands that we develop a variety of cultural representations which in turn dictate different ritual sensitivities. Our struggle today to become a "church in the modern world" coincides with a dramatic drop-off in sacramental confession, perhaps because it is increasingly difficult, in the face of such social upheaval, to say what, in our age, constitutes faithful discipleship. It is also a fact, whatever their strengths and weaknesses, that the revised rites have not yet been implemented in most of the United States and have not yet been sufficiently tested in pastoral practice to make definitive judgments about their merits. With all of these caveats, we begin dialogue with some of the theological emphases in the praenotanda to the *Rite of Penance*.

The document begins with "The Mystery of Reconciliation in the History of Salvation"

The Mystery of Reconciliation in the History of Salvation

(paragraphs 1–2). In summary, this section states the following: God's desire to reconcile humankind to Godself, made tangible in the prophets' cries and in John's preaching, is most perfectly manifest in Christ, sacrament of God's longing; this remains the task and the calling of those who follow Christ. Baptism, eucharist and penance are three unique ways in which the community of the church declares Christ's victory over sin in word and in ritual action.

These lines suggest to me a cluster of theological themes around the choice of the word *reconciliation* as the controlling metaphor of this sacrament: that reconciliation is God's work; that reconciliation presupposes relationship; that relationship with God is the key to defining sin; that one's experience of God profoundly affects the quality of that relationship as well as one's desire and ability to be reconciled. Furthermore, this first section of the praenotanda urges the question of the distinct role of the sacrament of reconciliation in the church's sacramental life.

Reconciliation as the Controlling Metaphor

One cannot help but marvel at the pervasive use of the word *reconciliation* throughout the praenotanda: Both the nature and the effect of the sacrament are captured in this word. Indeed, when the rite was first published, commentators were quick to point out the shift from an emphasis on confession or penance — placing stress on the action of the penitent (the *doing* of penance, the *telling* of sins) — to reconciliation, which places stress, in the first instance, on God and God's action in Christ. Paul captures the gist of it in Romans:

> For if while we were enemies, we were reconciled to God through the death of his Son, much more surely, having been reconciled, will we be saved by his life. But more than that, we even boast in God through our Lord Jesus Christ, through whom we have now received reconciliation.[8]

It may be impossible to comprehend how radical is the shift of the controlling metaphor of this sacrament. Reconciliation is an invitation to plunge into the abyss of God's mercy, goodness, love, healing and forgiveness, to deepen our friendship with the one who has been called "irrevocably welcoming, imperturbably forgiving and indestructibly reconciling."[9]

But, as I was challenged once from the floor after giving a talk about this: "Fine for you to say, but who else knows that!" Why is it that we have succeeded in communicating that Christian initiation is not about mastering a curriculum of dogmatic instruction but falling in love with a person, and yet we have not effected a similar shift in reconciliation — not helped people to look in the first instance to relationship, to God, grace and future, no longer simply to sin, self and past?

For what is sin if not the rupture of relationship with God, which disturbs and sometimes destroys God's plan for our destiny? Sin, the *Catechism of the Catholic Church* makes clear, can only be understood and appreciated for what it is if we *first* recognize that our destiny is to live in profound relationship with God, to seek God, to love God with our whole heart, soul, mind and strength. For only in this relationship "is the evil of sin unmasked in its true identity as humanity's rejection of God and opposition to [God], even as it continues to weigh heavy on human life and history."[10] Relationship is that which defines us as truly human; communion with God is our vocation; growing in our friendship with God is the work of a lifetime. Sin, then, is anything that weakens, denies or destroys our relationship with God.

> Perhaps the best way to speak of sin is to see it as the antithesis of our most grand and noble possibility. We understand the danger of sin and the seriousness of sin when we appreciate what it denies and what it destroys. Sin would be inconsequential if there were not something beautiful and tremendously graced in us that can be lost. Sin would be trifling if there were not some wonderful promise we were

meant to fulfill. The tragedy of sin is not only its particular wickedness or evil but also what is lost because of it: our true selves, our relationship with God and others, our happiness and peace.[11]

In light of our vocation to live in love with God and in harmony with all God's gifts, we are unambiguous in naming as "sin" everything that destroys our friendship with God. What our culture might otherwise excuse as "a developmental flaw, a psychological weakness, a mistake or the necessary consequences of an inadequate social structure,"[12] we cannot dismiss. Sin is not simply about breaking particular laws but about wounding our most fundamental relationship.

So reconciliation, too, must be about the work of repairing relationship with God in and through the mediation of the community. In that light, one's developing experience of God and the nurturing of such communion throughout a lifetime matters profoundly. But what if I have no relationship with God to speak of, no felt sense of God's presence in my life or only a vague sense of who God is? Or what if the God of my childhood no longer serves me well? Or what if the only thing I experience is distance and otherness, a detached and uncaring God who permits suffering and evil around me, which affects me and touches the people I love? I sometimes wonder if many people cannot believe either in the reality and gravity of sin or in reconciliation because it demands that we be in relationship with God, that God be real to us, that God be known to us, that the God of our Lord Jesus Christ become our God too. And since it is each one of us who makes God tangible and who embodies, or not, the forgiving Christ, the quality of our own conversion and our common life will determine whom we call to conversion, whose friendship with God we nurture as well as whose experience of God we distort. Furthermore, some will never believe in reconciliation — will never imagine the grace — because our categories for membership in the one body, with clear and impermeable boundaries, determine whom we censor in and whom we censor out.

Here's another concern: Our images of God are changing. We have discovered that the way we name God matters because the language we employ also names ourselves and identifies the relationship between God and us. If, for example, I believe that God is Father, Lord, King or Judge, my notion of God will name me child, servant, subject or defendant with all the attendant behavior that these respective images convey. But what of women whose God is Sophia Wisdom, Lover or Friend? What of the poor whose God is Deliverer, Emancipator, Liberator from Suffering? How often do these metaphors find place in our ritual prayer? Clearly, we need to recognize that large numbers of people in the community will have difficulty with both the concept and the experience of reconciliation because they have difficulty with the relationship upon which it is predicated, the language borrowed from human experience to capture the mystery or the incarnation of God in the community of those who claim to be God's disciples.

Finally, a footnote to this discussion on the metaphor of reconciliation: It could not have been more timely, given the state of our world. Separation, alienation, isolation, segregation, exclusion, estrangement, division, divorce — these are words that characterize the age in which we live. Reconciliation is their antithesis. Yet I think we have not yet imagined what a new emphasis on reconciliation might mean within and beyond our community for the sake of our world.

> [W]e are in need of reestablishing a genuine, vital and happy relationship with God, of being reconciled in humility and in love with [God]. From this first and constitutive harmony, the entire world of our experience can then be the expression of a need for reconciliation and can have its full impact in charity and justice to other persons in whom we will immediately acknowledge the right to be called our brothers and sisters. Reconciliation then can develop in other limitless and real spheres of existence: the community of the church itself, society, politics, ecumenism, peace.[13]

Reconciliation is like a seamless garment (to use a local Chicago metaphor),[14] potentially transforming every sphere.

Reconciliation in the Sacramental Economy

Another issue raised by the first section of the praenotanda is that of the place of reconciliation in the whole of the sacramental economy, and more specifically, the relationships among the several sacraments of reconciliation. Baptism, eucharist and penance are named in the praenotanda. But have we really attempted to articulate their relationship, especially the relationship between eucharist and penance?

Reconciliation begins when a person is incorporated into the body of Christ at baptism. It is maintained and strengthened each time we gather at the table of the eucharist. Indeed, it is virtually axiomatic to speak of the eucharist as the primary sacrament of reconciliation. But does this not imply that eucharist is also the ordinary, recurring, even daily sacrament of reconciliation? Accordingly, would we not see the several rites of sacramental reconciliation as extraordinary rites — never intended as frequent, devotional celebrations but rather available from time to time and celebrated sparingly when a penitent experiences serious sin, that is, a serious rupture in relationship with God, others, self or the earth for which some extraordinary remedy is needed?[15] An important corollary argument is this: If eucharist is conceived as the primary sacrament of reconciliation, then we cannot exclude from the table on the basis that those we would send away need first to be reconciled. Unreconciled penitents were welcomed to the table in the ancient church. Is it possible to replicate that welcome today?

The next section (paragraphs 3–7) of the praenotanda is "The Reconciliation

The Reconciliation of Penitents in the Church's Life

of Penitents in the Church's Life." Here we find an explanation of how the church exercises the ministry of reconciliation entrusted to us by Christ. The sacrament and its several constitutive elements are described: conversion, contrition, confession, satisfaction and absolution. In conclusion, the importance and benefits of frequent confession are noted.

Let me address three major theological issues prompted by this section of the praenotanda: the many modes of reconciliation in the church's life, our solidarity in sin and conversion, and the thorny question, What if it is the church itself which is sinful?

Many Modes of Reconciliation

Believers have always recognized that there are a variety of ways to do penance and be reconciled.[16] Our sensitivity to this reality is no less acute in this age. In 1987 a survey about penance and reconciliation was sent to all U.S. bishops, a nationwide random sample of priests, and representative active laity in three dioceses.[17] In summarizing the results, Francis Buckley reported that

> Believers have a deeper appreciation of other means of forgiveness: prayer, eucharist, alms (acts of charity to others), fasting (self-control), attempts to repair damage; apology; prayer groups and basic communities which provide opportunities to discuss challenges; spiritual direction and private retreats; communal reconciliation services; the sacrament for the sick; healing Masses.[18]

This is the experience of vast numbers of those whom we have called "core Catholics," good people who recognize in their daily experience and in the people they meet the healing and reconciling presence of God. It is a point to which we shall return in discussing who are today's ministers of reconciliation. Here it must suffice simply to note that these many actions and others like them need to be seen as part of the community's ordinary experience of reconciliation; their relationship to individual or communal reconciliation, strictly speaking, needs to be discovered and named, not ignored or discounted. If sacraments are understood in a process model, these many and varied experiences of reconciliation may be situated within the larger sacramental complex, and particular rituals to mark the various stages of the conversion journey also need to be identified.

Solidarity in Sin and Salvation

God finds us and saves us in a common life. Just as sin is inescapably a wound in the body of Christ, so the journey of conversion takes place in the midst of the community and most often through its mediation. Reconciliation is not a solitary endeavor but is dependent on what we might call the mutual ministry of the community. Thus far, the theology of the praenotanda on our solidarity in sin and salvation reflects traditional teaching.

What is new in this development of human solidarity is its introduction of the category of social sin, the joining of women and men in acts of injustice, whether actively or passively, whether in reference to what we have done or what we have failed to do. In addition, the very acknowledgment of social sin is the *raison d'etre* for communal penance, a communal rite of reconciliation and a commitment to work together for justice and peace.

A Sinful Church

But what of those instances when it is the church that is sinful, when it is the church itself in its policies, its repressions and its exclusions that has caused rupture? What of those instances when the church has remained silent or when it has participated in duplicitous behavior?

Robert Schreiter raises such questions in his book *Reconciliation: Mission and Ministry in a Changing Social Order*. It is true, he notes, that the church since the time of Paul has taken on the mantle of reconciliation, for example, calling warring parties to peace, working toward the end of alienation, pulling down the walls of hostility. Nevertheless, we cannot assume that the church has an absolute right to exercise the ministry of reconciliation.

> By its intimate bond with its Master, and as a mediator of God's grace, the church may well have an abstract right to the ministry of reconciliation, but the church may historically forfeit that right in circumstances where it has been part of the problem. And it must be admitted that all too often the church itself has been on the side of the oppressor in situations that afterward cry out for reconciliation.[19]

Using the crisis in South Africa as an example, Schreiter suggests that the church may sometimes promote negotiation while ignoring a prior call to justice; it may preach individual conversion while not dismantling sinful and oppressive social structures; it may decry violence but limit itself only to certain kinds of violence — that of the oppressed, for example, and not of the oppressors. In such situations it is obvious that while the church has a ministry of reconciliation, it is also in need of the exercise of that ministry within the larger society.[20]

Furthermore, within our own walls there are instances when it is the church itself which is in need of the ministry of reconciliation. When Cardinal Joseph Bernardin was first appointed to the archdiocese of Chicago, he decided to televise a mission during Holy Week. The single most effective moment in four evenings of prime-time viewing was the opening: Bernardin began by asking forgiveness of the community for the times when the church and its ministers had alienated the community, when false guilt was prompted by overzealous teachers, when insensitive confessors had not mediated Christ's healing and peace, when the church and its structures had been the occasion for scandal, disillusionment, rupture and pain in the lives of the community. Much was said by the Cardinal in the balance of that week, but little else was talked about afterward. It was a powerful experience for a local church to hear its leader acknowledge the church's sinfulness. For many it was the occasion for the beginning of reconciliation.

James Lopresti uses the term "prophetic alienation" to identify those who

> take a stance over against the community because of what they claim to be the community's own failure or sin. In its classic forms, such alienation resulted in schism, the separation of the churches. In contemporary forms, while schism may not be publicly acknowledged, that is the private experience of the prophetically alienated. In the past, doctrinal or juridical questions may have caused the separation. Today it is usually a matter of disagreement abut moral principles, the acceptability of variant lifestyles, or disputes over roles of church leadership.[21]

I appreciate Lopresti's identification of these prophets in our midst, but the hermeneutic of suspicion makes me wonder, as did Margaret Mitchell, why one who has been prophetically alienated would participate in "a mutual discovery of the sin of separation and the mutual desire for reunion."[22] Perhaps I find in this suggestion a reconciliation that is too facile: The hasty peace, the truce, the managed process are all ways that prophecy is muted, justice is ignored and reconciliation can be distorted and falsified.[23] Meanwhile, many with prophetic insight have experienced the lie and have given up on the institution altogether. They have gone away sad.

I turn now to a third section of the praenotanda, "Offices and Ministries in the Reconciliation of

Offices and Ministries in the Reconciliation of Penitents

Penitents" (paragraphs 8–11). In this section the topics treated are the role of the community in the celebration of penance and the dispositions required of ministers of reconciliation and of penitents.

This section makes us pose the question: Who is the minister of reconciliation? Who is the celebrant? One of the exceptional statements in the praenotanda is that faithful Christians, as they experience and proclaim the mercy of God, celebrate with the priest the liturgy by which the church continually renews itself. Here reconciliation is actually described as a *concelebration* of penitent and minister.

But what of the role of the community? One of the theological principles which was to guide the revision was that the entire Christian community works together for the conversion of sinners. *How* this happens is substantially ignored in the praenotanda, in subsequent commentaries and in current reflection and catechesis. The praenotanda states that "The whole church, as a priestly people, acts in different ways in the work of reconciliation entrusted to it by the Lord." Yet as this statement is developed, the role assigned to the community is largely that of intercession for sinners; even "calling sinners to repentance by preaching the word of God" is hedged in by canonical limitations.

Experience tells us, however, that many incidents of reconciliation happen in ordinary time with ordinary garden-variety believers:

> People already confess to laity: doctors, nurses, ministers to the sick, sisters, pastoral assistants, leaders of basic communities, friends, without obtaining absolution, but often fruitfully. They realize that absolution is not necessary.[24]

Where do we find the charism of reconciliation? Where do we experience God's healing presence? Where has the ethic of care been operative? Scores of individuals have reported their experience of reconciliation in spiritual direction, mentoring relationships, friendships, families and support communities of various kinds — and their experience they name "sacrament" while the church's official rites are largely ignored. What appears common in such experiences is the element of story-telling, the experience of acceptance — even affirmation and some embodied forgiveness.

Can't we develop a more active role for the community in the ministry of reconciliation, especially in light of Paul's famous charge to us: "All this is from God, who reconciled us to himself through Christ, and has given us the ministry of reconciliation; that is, in Christ, God was reconciling the world to himself, not counting their trespasses against them, and entrusting the message of reconciliation to us."[25] Should we not develop a clear theological position about the ministry of each member of the community that recognizes our ambassadorial role, that acknowledges and validates our human-religious experience that the need for reconciliation is ubiquitous and that the responsibility for healing and care belongs to all?

We speak easily of first conversion taking place step by step in the midst of the community, assisted by a variety of ministers with distinct roles and gifts. Surely second — and subsequent — conversion deserves the same. Our current absolution formula states that reconciliation happens "through the ministry of the church." Experience adds that God has been generous in distributing the charism of reconciliation, that there are many ministers, not all of them ordained presbyters. Could we not imagine trying to develop a spirituality of ministry true of all of us insofar as we have such gift and grace, and try to nurture this ministry broadly across the community?[26]

Under the title "The Celebration of the Sacrament of Penance" I will treat the next two divisions of the praenotanda (paragraphs 12 – 37)

The Celebration of the Sacrament of Penance

together to suggest my own bias that penitential celebrations are genuinely part of the whole sacramental process that we call reconciliation. These sections of the praenotanda describe the several forms of the sacrament of penance. The Western church of recent centuries has celebrated penance only in its individual form. There now are three distinct rites that complement one another and that make it possible to bring out the individual and communal aspects of penance, depending on circumstances, and to adapt the sacramental celebration to particular communities; or so the introduction states.

I would like to propose another analogy from initiation to illuminate the benefit of these several rites and suggest a way of deciding what should be celebrated at a given point in the life of an individual or a community. Shortly after the *Rite of Christian Initiation of Adults* was published, particularly because of the rigor of the journey of conversion and the personal faith which it entailed, some commentators began to question the practice of "indiscriminate infant baptism." The church was full of baptized pagans, they claimed. Perhaps baptism should be denied to infants if there is no evidence of faith on the part of parents or little hope that the child might be nurtured in the faith.

This wave of discussion was followed by another — an equal and opposite reaction — which stressed the place of the child in the Christian community and the utterly gratuitous love of God which infant baptism brings to ritual expression. Finally, a balance was recovered: We came to recognize that we needed to maintain the choice of infant and adult modes of initiation to highlight on the one hand God's initiative, election, free gift and unearned yet lavish relationship offered to us, and on the other hand, personal choice and free human response to God through the journey of conversion.

I think the same case could be made for the communal and individual rites, respectively: that communal rites allow God's utterly gratuitous healing and reconciliation to come to public visible expression, while individual rites might more clearly ritualize the personal, internal journey of conversion. Both are needed, and other forms besides,[27] to show the *many* faces of the merciful God who is our reconciliation and our lasting peace. One would decide on the appropriate form of celebration depending on what one experienced and needed to bring to ritual expression.

Key to that decision is an understanding of sin, of reconciliation and of the role of the community in the conversion of its members — the three elements named by the postconciliar Consilium as central theological issues.

Sin, however, is no longer susceptible to easy categorization. Mortal and venial are terms that seem evacuated of meaning except perhaps to those in the pre – Vatican II age cohort. As John Huels has observed:

> Few practicing Catholics today perceive themselves as having committed a sin so grave that they feel cut off entirely from God's grace. Hence they may not feel the urgency to go to individual confession, which is intended most particularly for the reconciliation of the serious sinner. The God proclaimed in today's church is more the loving and tender God of mercy rather than the severe and judgmental God who punishes sinners.[28]

At the same time, a sin may not be serious "objectively" but may be very troubling to the individual. This may be true especially for someone who has what was once referred to as a "delicate conscience" but now might be recognized as one who deeply cares about his or her relationship with God and others and is sensitive to whatever might rupture those relationships or lessen their love.

Perhaps, taking a cue from contemporary ethicists, the categories of personal sin and social sin might better name our experience today. Such a distinction will ultimately connect with "personal" and "communal" rites and may help to sort out the present confusion of these rites.

Finally, all ritual must be marked by honesty. This means that we must not celebrate healing, forgiveness or reconciliation prematurely. There is a line in T.S. Eliot's work: "We had the experience but missed the meaning." Our rites will not be honest stories honestly enacted if we move to ritual before there is something to celebrate.

Adaptations of the Rite

The final section of the praenotanda (paragraphs 38 – 40) covers adaptation of the rites of reconciliation to various regions and circumstances. Adaptations foreseen by the rite include translation of the texts, newly composed prayers, decisions about penitential gestures to manifest conversion and repentance in communal rites, the place of confession and the vesture to be worn. In addition, "priests are urged to determine the parts of the rite and the concrete modalities that are better suited on each occasion for the celebration of penance in its several forms, although they must always keep the basic structure of the rite and the formula of absolution and must follow the norms establish (sic) by the episcopal conference."[29]

Adaptation need not be belabored. A 1969 Roman document, *The Instruction on Translation of Liturgical Texts,* stated the case for adaptation succinctly:

> The prayer of the church is always the prayer of some actual community, assembled here and now. It is not sufficient that a formula handed down from some other time or region be translated verbatim, even if accurately, for liturgical use. The formula translated must become the genuine prayer of the congregation, and in it each of its members should be able to find and express himself or herself.[30]

Adaptation is a theological issue precisely because it is that necessary care to ensure the possibility of full, conscious and active participation, which means, for reconciliation, "the possibility of touching and being touched by God's life-affirming benevolence."

Everything said above can be summed up under the rubric of adaptation or, more accurately, inculturation. Inculturation of the rite of reconciliation must include recognition of changing God images and the attendant relationship they name and sustain; acknowledgment of changing patterns of frequency given the role of the eucharist and the variety of experiences of true, sacramental reconciliation in everyday life; acceptance of the reality that the church itself is sinful and in need of healing outside and within its walls; appreciation of the charism for healing and reconciliation which God has lavished among ordained and laity alike; and attentiveness to the distinct ritual demands of personal and social sin and reconciliation.

Conclusion

So, here we are, walking on the edge of two great abysses, a precarious journey at best. In drawing on that metaphor I didn't mean to sound apocalyptic; but I do mean to concur with the gravity of Paul VI's remarks about where our feet are planted and with his intimation about how high the stakes are in the choices we make. I would add that the stakes are also high in the issues we identify, whether anthropological or cultural or theological, since, as Paul VI noted, we are talking about the supreme interest of our life, our salvation.

I suspect by now that my theological bias is clear. Once, we emphasized the abyss of sin's lethal and fearsome depths. Today, if we must choose between the two great abysses, and perhaps counteract the recent past, I think we must lose ourselves for a time in the other abyss, that of God's tenderness, mercy, compassion and love. People who are overwhelmed by God's love become preoccupied with sustaining that relationship and with making God's tender mercy and compassion available to all. That, I believe, is the heart of reconciliation.

For Pastoral Reflection and Response

Kathleen Hughes has the wonderful and unsettling ability to raise provocative questions and issues. She makes us look again with a new lens or a fresh insight at what we thought we knew in order that we might gain a fuller understanding or ask a deeper question about the pastoral life of the church.

To take one example among many throughout her article: "Why is it that we have succeeded in communicating that Christian initiation is not about mastering a curriculum of dogmatic instruction but falling in love with a person, and yet we have not effected a similar shift in reconciliation — not helped people to look in the first instance to relationship, to God, grace and future, no longer simply to sin, self and past?" The pastoral question comes out of significant shifts in theological understanding: sacrament as process and not a moment, sin and grace as relational rather than discreet, objective acts. Just as initiation is the graced, communal process of making believers in disciples and lovers of Christ, reconciliation ought to be the graced, communal process of renewing, restoring and deepening believers as Christian disciples and lovers. In a process, relational view of sacramental reconciliation, what comprises sin and grace, death and resurrection in people's lives? How does such a view change our preaching, catechesis, spiritual direction, pastoral counseling, celebration of rites or forms of ministry? What is the meaning of discipleship? How do we present it?

Sacraments in a process model raise the crucial question of the link between people's experiences of reconciliation and the rituals and other ecclesial expressions of reconciliation. How do people recognize and name their sins and sinfulness? How do they seek and find reconciliation in their daily lives? How do they understand the interconnectedness of God, one another and all creation? How do these experiences and understandings compare and contrast with the church's? Can the church accept many reconciling activities as composing a reconciliation process? These are questions of the spiritual life, the way in which our life is related to God. As Dr. Hughes points out, images of God are twined with images of people: If God is Judge, I am defendant; if God is Father, I am child; if God is Lover, I am beloved; and so on. What images of God are woven into the fabric of people's lives? Is the range of images we present in all the church's activity wide enough and deep enough for redeemed sinners to interpret their experience and find meaning? Do the images relate only to individual identity (e.g., Judge/defendant), or do they also speak of community? If God is trinity, we are community; if God is mother hen, we are brood of chicks; if God is good shepherd, we are flock; if God is vine, we are branches and harvest of fruit.

What structures of our ecclesial life can foster spiritual growth? The process nature of reconciliation is enhanced for parishioners by reflective exercises that help name their ongoing conversion encounters, the development of companioning and communal discernment opportunities, and communal, scriptural reflection on Jesus' reconciling encounters. In addition, what models for social action will capture the imaginations of this generation, who have the desire to be ambassadors for justice, reconciliation and non-violence in a world that cries out for God's love? How does the quest for interdependence rather than codependence challenge church structures and models of leadership?

Ultimately it is the liturgical celebrations of the church that foster spiritual growth. Are our rites of reconciliation well celebrated? Do they mark the stages on the conversion journey? Is the language of the rites adequate to express the experiences people bring to their communal prayer? If not, what is a better language? What are ordinary and extraordinary rites of reconciliation in the ongoing conversion of believers? If eucharist is the ordinary and ongoing rite of reconciliation, ought we not see the extraordinary individual and communal rites as complementary, and expand the repertoire of these rites? In addition, adaptation to reflect the prayer and mode of reconciliation experienced by different cultures and races is critical for the spiritual growth of everyone in the Catholic community of North America.

The *Rite of Penance* remains one of the most powerful instruments for refounding the church today. It is a gold mine of wisdom about sacrament, church and ministry. And so one more pastoral recommendation: Replicate Kathleen Hughes' process in this article. Pastoral staffs, catechists, spiritual directors and social justice ministers need to sit down (again) with the praenotanda (*Rite of Penance*, 1–40) and study it for its theology and wisdom for pastoral practice. Let Hughes' questions guide you, and let your imagination take flight.

Finally a challenge back to Dr. Hughes (and, God rest him, Pope Paul VI): Are there two abysses or one? The alternatives of sin and grace, death and resurrection, seem to be sharp and clean. Is there not really one alienating abyss into which we all plunge, thanks to sin, only to find ourselves buoyed and salvaged by the gratuitous and merciful companionship of God-with-us, even in that deep pit?

The oral responses given at the symposium by Carol Gura, consultant on evangelization, reconciliation and adult spiritual development, Munson Township, Ohio, and Louis P. Sogliuzzo, SJ, director of Morristown Jesuit Retreat Center, Morristown, New Jersey, contributed greatly to these pastoral notes.

Notes

Introduction

1. Cardinal Joseph Bernardin, "New Rite of Penance Suggested," *Origins* 13:19 (October 20, 1983): 324–326.

2. James Lopresti, *Penance: A Reform Proposal for the Rite* (American Essays in Liturgy 6). (Collegeville: The Liturgical Press, 1987).

3. For descriptions of the parish implementation of the ReMembering model, see: Sarah Harmony, *ReMembering: The Ministry of Welcoming Alienated and Inactive Catholics* (Collegeville: The Liturgical Press, 1991), and Patrick J. Brennan, *The Reconciling Parish: A Process for Returning or Alienated Catholics* (Allen, Texas: Tabor Publishing, 1990).

1 Reconciliation in the Pastoral Context of Today's Church and World Does Reconciliation Have a Future?

1. See the special issue of *Time,* May 1, 1995, for an extensive report on the bombing of the Alfred P. Murrah Federal Building in Oklahoma City. The caption on page 5 for the cover story reads, "At 9:02 AM on April 19 [1995], a bomb destroyed the . . . Federal Building in Oklahoma City. Its scenes of carnage unleashed fear, anger, and sorrow across the nation — as well as an astonishingly swift quest for the suspected perpetrators of the slaughter. America had already learned to expect terror from beyond its borders. Now the country must deal with another reality: the monsters it has bred on its own."

2. United States Catholic Conference, *Brothers and Sisters to Us: U.S. Bishops' Pastoral Letter on Racism in Our Day,* November 14, 1979 (Washington, D.C.: USCC Office of Printing and Promotion Services, 1979), 3.

3. *Time* magazine, in a special issue, April 24, 1995, in its feature article beginning on page 22, records, "That was the case last week when Robert McNamara, Secretary of Defense under Kennedy and Johnson, expressed shame over America's conduct of the Vietnam War. Suddenly, hot arguments over the justice of that war resumed as if interrupted only by a pause for breath, rather than the passage of decades."

4. See David J. O'Brien and Thomas A. Shannon, eds., *Renewing the Earth: Catholic Documents on Peace, Justice, and Liberation* (Garden City: Doubleday and Company, 1977); John C. Haughey, *The Faith That Does Justice: Examining Christian Sources for Social Change* (New York: Paulist Press, 1977); Joseph Gremillion, *The Gospel of Peace and Justice: Catholic Social Teaching Since Pope John* (Maryknoll: Orbis, 1977).

5. James Lopresti, "RCIA and Reconciling the Alienated," in Robert J. Kennedy, ed., *Reconciliation: The Continuing Agenda* (Collegeville: The Liturgical Press, 1987), 159–170.

6. Robert J. Kennedy, "Baptism, Eucharist, and Penance: Theological and Liturgical Connections," in Robert J. Kennedy, ed., *Reconciliation*, 43–52.

7. Eucharistic Prayer for Masses of Reconciliation I.

8. James Dallen, "Recent Documents on Penance and Reconciliation," in Robert J. Kennedy, ed., *Reconciliation*, 103.

9. John Paul II, *Reconciliation and Penance*, December 2, 1984 (Washington, D.C.: USCC Office of Publishing and Promotion Services, 1985), 13. Italics mine.

10. James Dallen, "Reconciliation in the Sacarament of Penance," *Worship* 64:5 (September 1990): 386. Italics mine.

11. Matthew 18:20.

12. For an abbreviated description of the meaning of "womanist," see Toinette M. Eugene, "Womanist Theology," in Donald W. Musser and Joseph L. Price, eds., *A New Handbook of Christian Theology* (Nashville: Abingdon, 1992), 510–512. For a more extensive understanding of womanist ethics, see Katie G. Cannon, *Black Womanist Ethics* (Atlanta: Scholars' Press, 1989). For a particularly relevant contextual essay on this topic, see Diana L. Hayes, "Feminist Theology, Womanist Theology: A Black Catholic Perspective," in James H. Cone and Gayraud S. Wilmore, eds., *Black Theology: A Documentary History, Volume Two: 1980–1992* (Maryknoll: Orbis, 1993), 325–335.

13. James Dallen, "Reconciliation in the Sacrament of Penance," 389.

14. *Lumen Gentium*, 48. For other references to the church as the basic sacrament in the documents of Vatican Council II, see *Constitution on the Sacred Liturgy*, 5, 26 (and equivalently, 2); *Lumen Gentium*, 1, 9; *Ad Gentes*, 1, 5; *Gaudium et Spes*, 45.

15. Genesis 2:5 — 3:24.

16. This section of the paper is heavily indebted to the thoughts and words of Robert J. Hater, "Sin and Reconciliation: Changing Attitudes the Catholic Church," *Worship* 59:1 (January 1985): 18–31, for concepts and clarification of Kingdon of God and reconciliation themes.

17. Kingdom of God is used only in Wisdom 10:10, but its equivalent, "kingdom of Yahweh," is found in various places in the Hebrew Scriptures. See *Encyclopedic Dictionary of the Bible*, "Kingdom of God," 1269–1272.

18. The "kingdom" theme is developed especially in the preaching of Jesus, as recounted in the synoptic gospels. Cf. Mathew 5:20, 18:3; Luke 17:20ff. It is also found in Acts (14:22; 20:25) and especially in Paul (1 Thessalonians 2:12; I Corinthians 6:9).

19. See *Encyclopedic Dictionary of the Bible*, "Sin," 2219; "hata" means to miss the mark or fail (Genesis 41:9; Exodus 9:27); "awon" signifies a crooked deed; "pesa" means a revolt against God (Exodus 23:21).

20. Israel's infidelity (sin) was linked with the covenant promise to the Hebrew people (Hosea 1–3; Isaiah 54:6; Jeremiah 3:1–4). At the same time, the Hebrew people acknowledged the sins of individuals. In Genesis 3:3 we see the sin of Adam and Eve as the prototype of all individual sins. The sinner needs to be forgiven by God (Leviticus 4:20, 5:10; Numbers 14:19).

21. Mark 1:25; Matthew 9:13 and 5:14ff.; John 8:1–11; Hebrews 6:6; 2 Peter 2:20.

22. Cf. 2 Corinthians 5:18ff.; Collosians 1:20. Cf. "Reconciliation and Forgiveness," *National Bulletin on Liturgy* 9 (1976): 1–64.

23. M. Shawn Copeland, PHD, is an African American Catholic theologian currently appointed to the faculty of Marquette University in Milwaukee, Wisconsin. An account of her significant contributions as well as those of other Black Catholic theological scholars to the development of contemporary Black Catholic theology can be found in her article "African American Catholic and Black Theology: An Interpretation," in Gayraud S. Wilmore, ed., *African American Religious Studies: An Interdisciplinary Anthology* (Durham: Duke University Press, 1989), 228–248.

24. See Toinette M. Eugene and James N. Poling, *Balm for Gilead: Pastoral Care for African American Families Experiencing Abuse* (Nashville: Abingdon, forthcoming); and Toinette M. Eugene, *Lifting As We Climb: A Womanist Ethic of Care* (Nashville: Abingdon, forthcoming).

25. Toni Morrison, *Beloved* (New York: Alfred A. Knopf, 1987), 87ff.

26. James Lopresti, *Penance: A Reform Proposal for the Rite* (American Essays in Liturgy 6) (Collegeville: The Liturgical Press, 1987), 4–5.

27. Ibid., 5. Italics are mine.

28. This section of the paper is heavily indebted to the thoughts and words of James Lopresti's work on "Penance: A Reform Proposal for the Rite" in order to offer further expanded reflections on reconciliation in the pastoral context of today's church and world.

29. Ibid., 7.

30. Ibid., 11.

31. For an extended and extensive understanding of womanist ethics of care, see Toinette M. Eugene, "On Difference and the Dream of Pluralist Feminism," *Journal of Feminist Studies in Religion* 8:2 (fall 1992): 91–98; "To Be of Use," 138–147; "Two Heads are Better than One: Feminist and Womanist Ethics in Tandem," *Daughters of Sarah* 19:3 (summer 1993): 1, 6–11; "Swing Low, Sweet Chariot: A Womanist Response to Sexual Abuse and Violence," *Daughters of Sarah* 20:3 (summer 1994): 10–14; "No Defect Here: A Black Roman Catholic Womanist Reflection on a Spirituality of Survival," in Miriam Therese Winter, Adair Lummis, Allison Stokes, eds., *Defecting in Place: Women Claiming Responsibility for Their Own Spiritual Lives* (New York: Crossroad, 1994), 217–220.

32. Luke 4:18ff.

33. The *Kairos Document: Challenge to the Church*, 2d. rev. ed. (New York: Wm. B. Eerdmans Publishing Company and Theology in Global Context Association), 1987.

34. This section of the paper is heavily indebted to the thought and words of Mark Kline Taylor's *Remembering Esperanza: A Cultural-Political Theology for North American Praxis* (Maryknoll: Orbis, 1990), 175–242.

35. See Toinette M. Eugene, "On Difference and the Dream of Pluralist Feminism"; for further references in understanding distinctions of "difference," see Maria C. Lugones, "Hablando Cara a Cara/Speaking Face to Face: An Exploration of Ethnocentric Racism," in Gloria Anzaldua, ed., *Making Face Making Soul — Haciendo Caras: Creative*

and Critical Perspectives by Women of Color (San Francisco: Aunt Lute, 1990), 46 – 54; Elizabeth V. Spelman, *Inessential Woman: Problems of Exclusion in Feminist Thought* (Boston: Beacon Press, 1988).

36. For a critical and contextual understanding of dominance from a womanist perspective, see Patricia Hill Collins, *Black Feminist Thought: Knowledge, Consciousness, and the Politics of Empowerment* (London: HarperCollins, 1990).

For Pastoral Reflection and Response

1. Robert J. Schreiter, *Reconciliation: Mission and Ministry in a Changing Social Order* (Maryknoll: Orbis Books, 1992).

2. See *Rite of Christian Initiation of Adults,* 5.

Alienation in the Catholic Church Today Evidence from the Catholic Pluralism Project

1. James D. Davidson, "Identity and the Various Subcultures Found in the Church Today," in *Evangelization, Culture and Catholic Identity,* by William B. Friend, James D. Davidson, Angela A. Zukowski and Michael J. Himes (St. Leo, Florida: St. Leo College Press, 1996), 45 – 60; and Andrea S. Williams and James D. Davidson, "Catholic Conceptions of Faith: A Generational Analysis," *Journal of the Sociology of Religion* (1996).

2. We actually had a 62 percent return rate but had to delete five percent of the cases when we discovered that some wives had returned questionnaires for their husbands and some husbands had filled them out for their wives. Deleting these cases reduced the return rate but improved the accuracy of the findings.

3. A full report of the findings of the Catholic Pluralism Project is found in James D. Davidson, Andrea S. Williams, Richard A. Lamanna, Jan Stenftenagel, Kathleen Maas Weigert, William Whalen, and Patricia Wittberg, *The Search for Common Ground: What Unites and Divides Catholic Americans* (Huntington, IN: Our Sunday Visitor, 1997).

4. The overall correlation between self-concepts and self-interests is positive (r = .66, that is, there is a 43 percent overlap of the two dimensions). However, there are some individuals who have strong Catholic identities who do not report many benefits from being Catholic, and persons who have relatively weak religious identities but derive many benefits from being in the church. We are examining the social correlates of these circumstances in separate analyses.

5. Dean R. Hoge, *Converts, Dropouts, Returnees: A Study of Religious Change among Catholics* (Washington: United States Catholic Conference, and New York: The Pilgrim Press, 1981).

6. William V. D'Antonio, James D. Davidson, Dean R. Hoge and Ruth A. Wallace, *American Catholic Laity in a Changing Church* (Kansas City: Sheed and Ward, 1989); and *Laity American and Catholic: Transforming the Church* (Kansas City: Sheed and Ward, 1996).

7. Albert Bandura, *Social Learning Theory* (Englewood Cliffs, New Jersey: Prentice-Hall, 1977); and *Social Foundations of Thought and Action: A Social Cognitive Theory* (Englewood Cliffs, New Jersey: Prentice-Hall, 1986).

The Wounded Soul Through the Lens of Pastoral Psychology

1. Sharon Parks, *The Critical Years: The Young Adult Search for a Faith to Live By* (San Francisco: Harper & Row, 1986), 43ff.

2. Antoine Vergote, *Guilt and Desire: Religious Attitudes and Their Pathological Derivatives* (New Haven and London: Yale University Press, 1988). See also John Gallagher, *The Basis for Christian Ethics* (Mahwah, NJ: Paulist, 1985), 55ff.

3. Ibid., 44.

4. See Hans G. Furth, *Knowledge as Desire: An Essay on Freud and Piaget* (New York: Columbia University Press, 1987), 57ff. Also, Calvin S. Hall, *A Primer of Freudian Psychology* (New York: Mentor, 1979), 109: "This state of affairs in which the boy craves exclusive sexual possession of the mother and feels antagonistic toward the father is called the *Oedipus complex.* Oedipus was a prominent figure in Greek mythology who killed his father and married his mother. When the boy renounces the mother, he may either identify with the lost object, his mother, or intensify his identification with his father. Which of these will occur depends upon the relative strength of the masculine and feminine components in the constitutional make-up of the boy."

5. See the explanation of female oedipal development in Carol Gilligan, *In a Different Voice: Psychological Theory and Women's Development* (Cambridge, Mass.: Harvard University Press, 1982), 5ff. Gilligan (p. 8) cites Nancy Chodorow, *The Reproduction of Mothering* (Berkeley: University of California Press, 1978), 167: ". . . [B]ecause they are parented by a person of the same gender . . . girls come to experience themselves as less differentiated than boys, as more continuous with and related to the external object-world, and as differently oriented to their inner object-world as well."

   A teacher friend of mine who reviewed this paper observed that day-care children risk falling outside the dynamics of the classical oedipal analysis. As they grow into school-age children, they often have a poor self-image, an insensitive dominance over other children rather than an attraction to cooperation, and a psychological relation with both parents that is severed by the functional absence of the parents as emotional continents in their lives at the time that parental love should be most decisive. Such dynamics will surely have some bearing upon the child's development of an understanding of sin.

6. Jean Piaget, *The Moral Judgment of the Child* (New York: The Free Press, 1965).

   Anger is another factor in the dynamics of conscience formation. Children and youth are expected to be chaste. Sexual frustration leads to resentment. Our society's failure to communicate persuasive reasons for childhood and adolescent chastity contributes to youth's anger at social norms and at parents and other authority figures.

   The denial of sexual expression and the difficulty young people have in learning how to negotiate meaningful adult relationships promote youth's projecting onto others responsibility for the difficulties of their growth into sexual maturity. In mature relations, love neutralizes the hostility of resentment. But where intersexual relationships are uniformly frustrating, hostility frequently erupts into violence (or passive-aggressive transformations of violence and resentment). Freud's intuition that sex and violence go together (in the sense that people respond violently to having their sexual drives frustrated) appears to be verified in the way our culture behaves.

7. Vergote, op cit., 44; cf. 93ff.

8. See P.J. Philibert, "Symbolic and Diabolic Images of God," *Studies in Formative Spirituality*, XI: 1 (February 1985): 87–101.

9. *The Catechism of the Catholic Church* (USCC, 1994) reaffirms the traditional teaching in paragraphs 2351–2356. The catechism nuances this traditional teaching in 2342: "Self-mastery is a long and exacting work. One can never consider it acquired once and for all. It presupposes renewed effort at all stages of life."

10. Vergote, op. cit., 74. Moreover: "The culpabilization of the instincts tends to exalt the passive virtues of obedience, renunciation, and humility. . . . Of course pride is universally abhorrent, but a heavy emphasis on obedience deadens initiative, just as an exaggerated idealization of renunciation poisons joy and an insistence on humility paralyzes man's creative forces." (77)

11. *The Catechism*, 1617, states: "Since [Christian marriage] signifies and communicates grace, marriage between baptized persons is a true sacrament of the New Covenant." Cf. 1609–1616.

12. Piaget, op. cit. 84ff.

13. Cited in Carl Rogers and Barry Stevens, *Person to Person* (New York: Pocket Books, 1971), 25.

14. Erikson calls this quality "intimacy." See Erik H. Erikson, *Insight and Responsibility* (New York: Norton, 1964), 127ff. Also P.J. Philibert, "Readiness for Ritual" *Alternative Futures for Worship, Vol. I* (Collegeville, MN: Liturgical Press, 1987), 103–4.

15. St. Thomas Aquinas, *Summa Theologiae*, vol. 16 (1a2ae. 1–5), ed. Thomas Gilby (New York: McGraw-Hill, 1969), 3ff.

16. The goal of "good enough" understanding and freedom is borrowed from object relations theorists; like them, I wish to avoid utopian expectations for human self-expression and yet do wish to maintain the ideal of the nobility of the moral person. For further explanation, see John McDargh, *Psychoanalytic Object Relations Theory and the Study of Religion* (Lanham, MD: University Press of America, 1983).

17. Concerning catharsis, the following is interesting: "Breuer's and Freud's method of treatment, moreover, bore a uniquely rational relationship to their conception of the disorder. If the patient, usually under light hypnosis but sometimes without it, could be brought to reexperience the affect that had been suppressed in the first instance, then the symptoms would disappear. This method — named 'cathartic therapy,' somewhat imprecisely after Aristotle's theory of the purgative value of viewing tragedy in the theater — was soon tried by a number of physicians in other cities, generally with a view of comparing it with more standard forms of hypnotism." John Kerr, *A Most Dangerous Method: The Story of Jung, Freud, and Sabina Spielrein* (New York: Knopf, 1993), 37.

18. Josef Goldbrunner, *Individuation: A Study of the Depth Psychology of Carl Gustav Jung* (Notre Dame: University of Notre Dame Press, 1964), 119ff.

19. Dietrich Bonhoeffer, *Ethics* (London, SCM Press, 1955), 332: "From these considerations it becomes evident that the essential character of the lie is to be found at a far deeper level than in the discrepancy between thought and speech. One might say that the man who stands behind the word makes his word a lie or a truth."

20. James Lopresti suggests something parallel to these three categories with his own proposal of three types that he calls "the unawakened, the alienated, and the prophetically alienated" in *Penance: A Reform Proposal for the Rite* (American Essays in Liturgy 6) (Washington, DC: The Pastoral Press, 1987), 11–19.

21. William Johnston: *The Inner Eye of Love: Mysticism and Religion* (San Francisco: Harper & Row, 1978), 127. See discussion of this passage in Raymond Studzinski, *Spiritual Direction and Midlife Development* (Chicago: Loyola University Press, 1985), 20ff.

Are Anthropological Crises Contagious? Reflexivity, Representation, Alienation and Rites of Penance

1. James Lopresti, *Penance: A Reform Proposal for the Rite* (American Essays in Liturgy 6) (Washington: The Pastoral Press, 1987).

2. Mikhail Bakhtin, *Problems of Dostoevsky's Poetics* (Minneapolis: University of Minnesota Press, 1984), 70.

3. Lopresti, op.cit., 8–9.

4. Clifford Geertz, *Works and Lives: The Anthropologist as Author* (Stanford, California: Stanford University Press, 1988), 9.

5. Ibid., 5.

6. Ibid., 10.

7. Talal Asad and John Dixon, "Translating Europe's Others," in *Europe and Its Others*, vol. 1, ed. Francis Barker, Peter Hulme, Margaret Iversen and Diana Loxley (Colchester: University of Essex Press, 1985), 170–193.

8. Bakhtin, op. cit.

9. Geertz, op. cit., 10.

10. Colin Turnbull, *The Forest People* (New York: Simon and Schuster, 1962); and *The Wayward Servants: The Two Worlds of African Pygmies* (Garden City, New York: Natural History Press, 1965).

11. The following are some of the seminal attempts to recognize that honesty in the representation of Others requires that the anthropologist as pilgrim (the Self on a quest) not be ignored or separated from the anthropologist as cartographer (the Self constructing academically defined forms of knowledge): Karen Brown, *Moma Lola: A Vodou Priestess in Brooklyn* (Berkeley: University of California Press, 1992); V. Crapanzano, *Tuhami: Portrait of a Moroccan* (Chicago: University of Chicago Press, 1980); L. Danforth, *The Death Rituals of Rural Greece* (Princeton: Princeton University Press, 1982); and Kevin Dwyer, *Moroccan Dialogues: Anthropology in Question* (Baltimore: Johns Hopkins University Press, 1982).

12. Deborah Tannen, *You Just Don't Understand: Women and Men in Conversation* (New York: Ballantine Books, 1991).

13. Talal Asad and John Dixon, art. cit., 173–174.

14. Pierre Bourdieu and Loic J. D. Wacquant, *An Invitation to Reflexive Sociology* (Chicago: University of Chicago Press, 1992), 69. Emphasis in the original.

15. Talal Asad and John Dixon, art. cit., 175.

16. Karen Brown. op. cit.

17. Ibid., 17–18.

18. Ibid., 14–15.

19. Brown quoting Clifford Geertz in ibid., 15.

20. Gananeth Obeyesekere, *Medusa's Hair: An Essay on Personal Symbols and Religious Experience* (Chicago: University of Chicago Press, 1981), 51. Emphasis added.

21. Katrina Clark and Michael Holquist, *Mikhail Bakhtin* (Cambridge: Harvard University Press, 1984), 5.

22. Michael Holquist, *Dialogism: Bakhtin and His World* (London: Routledge, 1990), 34. Emphasis in the original.

23. Mikhail Bakhtin, op. cit., 6. Emphasis in the original.

24. Ideally I would provide you with a "thick description" both of how I came to be there and of the event itself. (On "thick description," see Clifford Geertz, *The Interpretation of Cultures,* [New York: Basic Books, 1973].) I can only summarize here, but I refer you to my "Conversations among Liturgists," *Liturgy Digest* 2:2 (spring/summer 1995): 36–124.

25. James Lopresti, op. cit.

26. David Hess, *Science in the New Age: The Paranormal, Its Defenders and Debunkers, and American Culture* (Madison: The University of Wisconsin Press, 1993), 43. Emphasis in the original.

27. Keith H. Basso, *Portraits of "The Whiteman": Linguistic Play and Cultural Symbols among the Western Apache* (New York: Cambridge University Press, 1979).

28. Clifford Geertz, *Works and Lives,* 10.

29. David Hess, loc. cit.

30. If you want to see the degree to which Lopresti has incorporated this "community" in his essay — and how it becomes almost a mantra-like incantation — try circling, as I did, each use of the word, starting from page 19.

31. Clifford Geertz, *Works and Lives,* 4.

32. Mikhail Bakhtin, op. cit., 6. Emphasis in the original.

33. Robert Orsi, "'He Keeps Me Going': Women's Devotion to St. Jude Thaddeus and the Dialectics of Gender in American Catholicism 1929-1965," in *Belief in History: Innovative Approaches to European and American Religion,* ed. Thomas Kselman (Notre Dame: University of Notre Dame Press, 1991), 137–169.

34. Ibid., 155. Emphasis added.

35. Ibid., 158.

36. Ibid., 159.

37. Ibid., 160.

38. For example, Caroline Walker Bynam, "The Body of Christ in the Later Middle Ages: A Reply to Leo Steinberg," and "Women's Stories, Women's Symbols: A Critique of Victor Turner's Theory of Liminality," in *Fragmentation and Redemption: Essays on Gender and the Human Body in Medieval Religion* (New York: Zone Books, 1992), 79–117 and 27–51, respectively; Eamon Duffy, *The Stripping of the Altars: Traditional Religion in England 1400–1580* (New Haven: Yale University Press, 1992). Miri Rubin, *Corpus Christi: The Eucharist in Late Medieval Culture* (Cambridge: Cambridge University Press, 1991).

39. Caroline Walker Bynam, "Did the Twelfth Century Discover the Individual?" in *Jesus as Mother: Studies in the Spirituality of the High Middle Ages* (Berkeley: University of California Press, 1982), 82–109.

40. Caroline Walker Bynum, "The Body of Christ in the Later Middle Ages: A Reply to Leo Steinberg," loc. cit.

41. Caroline Walker Bynum, *Holy Feast and Holy Fast: The Religious Significance of Food to Medieval Women* (Berkeley: University of California Press), 1987.

42. Caroline Walker Bynum, "Women's Stories, Women's Symbols: A Critique of Victor Turner's Theory of Liminality," loc. cit.

43. James Clifford, *Maurice Leenhardt: Ethnologist and Missioner*, PHD dissertation, Harvard University, 1977; *Person and Myth: Maurice Leenhardt in the Melanesian World* (Berkeley: University of California Press, 1982).

44. James Clifford, *Person and Myth*, 84.

45. Ibid.

For Pastoral Reflection and Response

1. NCCB Pastoral Research and Practices Committee, "Reflections on the Sacrament of Penance in Catholic Life Today: A Study Document," *Origins* 19:38 (February 22, 1990): 617; Joseph Gremillion and Jim Castelli, *The Emerging Parish: The Notre Dame Study of Catholic Life Since Vatican II* (San Francisco: Harper and Row, 1987), 146.

2. Mark Chaves and James C. Cavendish, "More Evidence on U.S. Catholic Church Attendance," *Journal for the Scientific Study of Religion* 33:4 (1994): 376–381, and Thomas J. Sweetser, "The Parish: What Has Changed, What Remains?" *America* (February 17, 1996): 6.

3. NCBB, art. cit. 617.

4. This happy phrase is Mary Catherine Hilkert's from her article on preaching, "Naming Grace: A Theology of Proclamation," *Worship* 60:5 (September 1986): 434–449.

Paul's 1 Corinthians on Reconciliation in the Church
Promise and Pitfalls

1. Margaret M. Mitchell, *Paul and the Rhetoric of Reconciliation: An Exegetical Investigation of the Language and Composition of 1 Corinthians*, HUT 28 (Tubingen: J.C.B. Mohr/Paul Siebeck, 1991; American ed.: Louisville: Westminster/John Knox, 1993).

History and the Reform of Penance

1. *Constitution on the Sacred Liturgy [CSL]*, 4.

2. CSL, 23.

3. CSL, 23.

4. Schema 279; *De Paenitentia*, 6. The report was dated 16 March 1968. This preliminary material has not yet been published or analyzed.

5. Cyrille Vogel was presumably responsible for the Western history and Louis Ligier for the Eastern.

6. CSL, 72. An official interpretation given by Archbishop Hallinan indicated that "nature" referred to the social and ecclesial character of the sacrament. See *Acta Synodalia Sacrosancti Concilii Vaticani II* (Roma: Typis Polyglottis Vaticanis, 1962) 2, Part 2, 567.

7. e.g., the rigid discipline kept many people from entering penance until they were dying, but repentant sinners were allowed to share communion.

8. These included the place and manner of celebration, prayer in the celebration, posture and the priest's extended hands in absolving, several prayers of absolution (optative, declarative, deprecative), and, in particular, communal celebrations with common absolution after or without individual confessions. So-called "general" absolution (without previous individual confession) received particular attention, including a survey of Roman indults permitting it and of theological opinions regarding it.

9. For a discussion of history as a factor in the theology of penance, see Giles Pater, *Karl Rahner's Historico-Theological Studies on Penance: The Retrieval of Forgotten Truths* (unpublished PHD dissertation, University of Notre Dame, 1977), 4–59. In *The Order of Penitents: Historical Roots and Pastoral Future* (Collegeville, MN: Liturgical Press, 1988), 7–67, Joseph A. Favazza provides a detailed and clear survey of developing interpretations of the history.

10. This acknowledgment of variety, change, and development was also found in the later document from the International Theological Commission. The document, "Penance and Reconciliation," is available in *Origins* 13 (1984): 513–524, and in *International Theological Commission: Texts and Documents, 1969–1985* (San Francisco: Ignatius Press, 1989), 225-249. Pope John Paul II minimally recognizes historical development in his postsynodal apostolic exhortation, *Reconciliatio et paenitentia* (2 December 1984); see John Paul II, *Reconciliation and Penance* (Washington, D.C.: United States Catholic Conference), 30.

11. e.g., Ladislas Orsy in his *The Evolving Church and the Sacrament of Penance* (Denville, NJ: Dimension Books, 1978). In my opinion, Orsy oversimplifies the development in

his description of two systems, Mediterranean (31–34) and Irish (35–37), which came into conflict (37–42) and reached a compromise (42–46) which was later canonized by Lateran IV and Trent (46–48). I am more inclined to see a rapport between developments in canonical penance in Gaul and Irish adaptation of Eastern monastic penance, even though bishops at the time reacted against Irish "innovations."

12. As an example, Herbert Vorgrimler's *Busse und Krankensalbung* (Freiburg: Herder, 1978), probably the best history of the theology of penance in print, affirms that ancient penance was primarily oriented toward the penitent sinner's reconciliation with the church and accepts that private penance probably emerged in the West as an Irish adaptation of Eastern monastic practice.

13. The summary phrase "reconciliation with the church" is commonly used but requires nuancing. Serious sin, even that leading to segregation in the order of penitents, did not normally entail excommunication. Though penitents did have a distinct status, it was a status in the church and among the faithful. They were, however, forbidden, in varying degrees, to exercise their active role as members of the faithful and were especially prohibited from sharing eucharistic communion, the sign of full communion with the faithful in the church. But even this latter prohibition was not uniform, as we know of instances where unreconciled penitents were permitted to share eucharistic communion.

14. CSL, 9.

15. CSL, 10.

16. *Principles of Sacramental Theology,* 2d ed. (Westminster, MD: Newman Press, 1960), 385–431, especially 396–400, 424–431.

17. In *Lamentabili* (DS 3439–3440) and in *Pascendi* (DB 2088; omitted in DS).

18. *Catechism,* 1115–1116.

19. Our earliest evidence is primarily from Tertullian's *De paenitentia* and *De pudicitia.*

20. I have, to some extent, simplified the parallels to bring out the similarity between the order of catechumens and the order of penitents. In particular, it is not clear to what extent there was a rite of reconciliation (paralleling confirmation in the initiation process?) prior to the resolution of the penitential controversies.

21. Clergy, because of their existing status as members of a distinct *ordo*, were also generally not eligible to enter this transitional group. Prospective penitents who were married required their spouse's permission.

22. There is some similarity as well to the more recent practice of forbidding scrupulous persons to make a detailed confession.

23. Paul Galtier, "Pénitents et 'Converti': De la pénitence latine à la pénitence celtique," *Revue d'Histoire Ecclésiastique* 33 (1937): 5-26, 277-305.

24. For a detailed history and analysis, see Raffaele Pazzelli, *St. Francis and the Third Order: The Franciscan and Pre-Franciscan Penitential Movement* (Chicago: Franciscan Herald Press, 1989).

25. See Cyrille Vogel, "Le pélérinage pénitentielle," *Revue des Sciences religieuses* 38 (1964): 113–153; reprinted (with the same pagination) in *En rémission des péchés: Recherches sur les systémes pénitentiels dans l'Englise latine,* Alexandre Faivre, ed. (Aldershot: Variorum, 1994)

26. I have explored correlations of the lack of a ritual of reconciliation to developing Western spirituality in "The Absence of a Ritual of Reconciliation in Celtic Penance," in *The Journey of Western Spirituality* (A.W. Sadler, ed; Chico, CA: Scholars Press, 1981), 79–105, and in *The Reconciling Community*, 150–156.

27. The classic study is Amédée Teetaert, *La confession aux laïques dans l'Église latine depuis le Vllle jusqu'au XIVe siécle* (Paris: Gabalda, 1926).

28. See especially Anton Eppacher, "Die Generalabsolution: Ihre Geschichte (9–14 Jahrhundert) und die gegenwärtige Problematik im Zusammenhang mit den gemeinsamen Bussfeiern," *Zeitschrift für katholische Theologie* 90 (1968): 296–308, 385 –421. For a specific example, see Jorge Perales, "The Service of the Indulgentia: Light on the Rite of General Confession and Absolution," *Worship* 62 (1988): 138–153.

29. I would question the claim of the International Theological Commission and of Pope John Paul II in *Reconciliatio et Paenitentia* that the history of penance is the history of the personal dimension of the sacrament emerging into greater clarity. The claim neglects to take into account the differing socio-cultural contexts and assumes the primacy of individual confession and absolution. There is no evidence, for example, that ancient penance was impersonal.

30. For example, José Ramos-Regidor, "'Reconciliation' in the Primitive Church and Its Lessons for Theology and Pastoral Practice Today," *Concilium* 61 (1971): 76–88; Catherine Dooley, "The History of Penance in the Early Church: Implications for the Future," in *Reconciliation: The Continuing Agenda*, ed. Robert J. Kennedy (Collegeville, MN: Liturgical Press, 1987), 83–95.

31. In his 1984 post-synodal exhortation, Pope John Paul II claims that Vatican II's reform intention was to highlight Tridentine doctrine; see *Reconciliatio et Paenitentia*, 30. This contrasts sharply with the official relatio on the intent of the conciliar call for reform; see above, note 6.

32. Although "general absolution" is the term commonly used, it has come to be associated with emergency situations, such as when death is imminent. Individual reconciliation is impossible in such situations but so is the communal celebration. I prefer to speak of "communal" or "public" absolution in the context of communal celebrations to avoid the misleading connotation.

33. *Rite of Penance*, 8.

34. The Twelve Steps of Alcoholics Anonymous, Fifth Step.

35. 2 Corinthians 5:19.

36. 2 Corinthians 5:20.

37. See Joseph Bernardin, "New Rite of Penance Suggested," in *Origins* 13 (1983): 324-326; Robert Blondell, "A Possible Solution," in *Assembly* 10 (1983): 218–221; Joseph Slattery, "Restore the *Ordo Paenitentium?* — Some Historical Notes," in *The Living Light* 20 (1984): 248-253; James Lopresti, *Penance: A Reform Proposal for the Rite* (American Essays in Liturgy 6) (Washington, D.C.: Pastoral Press, 1987); Favazza, *Order of Penitents*, 253ff.

38. See especially Wolfgang Lentzen-Deis, *Busse als Bekenntnisvollzug: Versuch einer Erhellung der sakramentalen Bekehrung anhand der Bussliturgie des alten pontificals Romanum* (Freiburg: Herder, 1968).

39. *Rite of Penance,* 5.

40. *Rite of Penance,* 7.

41. *Rite of Penance,* 11.

42. 2 Corinthians 5:18–20.

Walking on the Edge of Two Great Abysses Theological Perspectives on Reconciliation

1. Paul VI, address to a general audience on the new rite of penance, 3 April 1974, *Documents on the Liturgy* [DOL], International Commission on English in the Liturgy (Collegeville: The Liturgical Press, 1982), 3110.

2. CSL, 72; DOL, 72.

3. Annibale Bugnini, *The Reform of the Liturgy* 1948–1975, trans. Matthew J. O'Connell (Collegeville: The Liturgical Press, 1990), 664.

4. Liturgists have sometimes speculated about the fact that the Second Vatican Council discussed liturgy first. We wonder about what its effect was in the development of later schema, and we wonder whether the *Constitution on the Sacred Liturgy* might have been developed differently, perhaps more attentive to the world church, for example, if it had time to mature after other conciliar statements were made. Perhaps we also might fruitfully speculate about what the reform of the *Rite of Penance* might have looked like if it had been the first rather than the last major ritual to be reformed after Vatican II. Might we detect already something of a siege mentality in this letter from the Sacred Congregation of Worship to the Pope in May 1971: "Dissatisfaction with this sacrament has now become general: On all sides we see new initiatives, studies, researches, study groups. Individual bishops and even episcopal conferences have published their own documents or are preparing them. Clarification from the central authority is becoming increasingly necessary and is increasingly expected, if only to avoid what are seen as abuses. . . . The matter must be dealt with immediately, and a good number of persons expert in the field must be assigned to it in order to enlighten pastors and faithful on this sensitive, complex, and vitally important subject before what is too late" (Bugnini, 670). One must wonder: Too late for what?

5. Annibale Bugnini, 665. While Bugnini only cites three principles, I have been told by James Dallen that there was a fourth principle identified by the concilium, namely, the place of penance in the Christian life.

6. Annibale Bugnini, 664–683 passim.

7. Annibale Bugnini, 674. The Congregation for the Doctrine of the Faith invariably opted for the more restrictive choice, sometimes completely ignoring the work of the *periti* and the Congregation for Divine Worship. In one case, "when asked what their reasons were, the Congregation replied that it would make them known to the Pope."

8. Romans 5:10–11.

9. Monika Hellwig, *Sign of Reconciliation and Conversion* (Wilmington, Delaware: Michael Glazier, Inc., 1982), 24.

10. *Catechism of the Catholic Church,* 386.

11. Paul Wadell, "Sin: Not the Way It's Supposed to Be," unpublished lecture, 7.

12. *Catechism*, 387.

13. Paul VI, address announcing the Holy Year 1975, 9 May 1973, DOL, 4071.

14. Cardinal Joseph Bernardin's teaching on the consistent ethic of life was often referred to as the "seamless garment" ethic.

15. Bill Cosgrove has stated that for nearly all of the church's long history, confession was a rare event. Only in the twentieth century, and largely as a result of Pius X's encouragement of more frequent communion, did confession become more frequent, and only in the 1950s had it increased to monthly and even weekly confession. He gives an interesting summary of reasons for the decline in confession's frequency today. See "The Decline of Confessions: Disaster or Return to Normal?" *The Furrow* 45:3 (March 1994): 158–162.

16. I remember once reading a medieval list of seven ways of doing penance which corresponded to the seven penitential psalms. I was a bit alarmed that one suggestion was martyrdom!

17. See *Origins* 19:38 (22 February 1990): 613–624.

18. Francis J. Buckley, "Recent Developments in Reconciliation: A Survey of Bishops, Clergy, and Laity about Penance and Reconciliation," in *The Living Light* 27:1 (Fall 1990): 38–39. See also Elaine Polomsky, "What Are Non-Confessing Catholics Doing with Their Guilt?" in *U.S. Catholic* 50 (April 1985): 30–36.

19. Robert J. Schreiter, *Reconciliation: Mission and Ministry in a Changing Social Order* (Maryknoll, New York: Orbis Books, 1992), 64.

20. Schreiter here makes use of the Kairos Document. See "The Kairos Document: Challenge to the Church," *Journal of Theology for South Africa*, 53 (1985): 61-81.

21. James Lopresti, *Penance: A Reform Proposal for the Rite* (American Essays in Liturgy 6) (Collegeville: The Liturgical Press), 10.

22. James Lopresti, 19.

23. See Robert J. Schreiter, 18–27.

24. Francis J. Buckley, 44.

25. 2 Corinthians 5:18–19.

26. See Robert Hater, "Sin and Reconciliation: Changing Attitudes in the Catholic Church," *Worship* 59 (1989): 18–31.

27. See Daniel P. Grigassy, "Nonsacramental Rites of Reconciliation: Forsaken or Disguised?" in *Liturgical Ministry* 4 (winter, 1995). Grigassy describes situations of victimization, addictions, alienation, ecumenism, immigration and diminishment, all of which, in his judgment, cry out for ritual pastoral care and reconciliatory practices.

28. John Huels, "Penance, Canon Law, and Pastoral Practice," *Liturgical Ministry* 4 (winter, 1995): 35.

29. Annibale Bugnini, 679.

30. DOL, 857.

Contributors

James Dallen, STD, is professor of religious studies at Gonzaga University in Spokane, Washington. A specialist in liturgy and sacramental theology, he is author of *The Reconciling Community: The Rite of Penance* (Pueblo, 1986); *The Dilemma of Priestless Sundays* (Liturgy Training Publications, 1994); and, with Joseph Favazza, *Removing the Barriers: The Practice of Reconciliation* (Liturgy Training Publications, 1991).

James D. Davidson Jr., PhD, is professor of sociology at Purdue University in West Lafayette, Indiana. His research and publications have been in the sociology of religion, social stratification, racial and ethnic groups and sports. He is coauthor, along with William D'Antonio, Dean Hoge and Ruth Wallace, of *American Catholic Laity in a Changing Church* (Sheed and Ward, 1989) and *Laity: American and Catholic: Transforming the Church* (Sheed and Ward, 1996). He is the principle author of *The Search for Common Ground: What Unites and Divides Catholic Americans* (Our Sunday Visitor, 1997), which presents the findings of the Catholic Pluralism Project.

Toinette M. Eugene, PhD, was, at the time of the meeting at which these papers were given, associate professor of Christian social ethics at Garrett-Evangelical Theological Seminary in Evanston, Illinois. She later accepted the dual position of formation director for the Pastoral Leadership Placement Board and director of the African American Pastoral Center of the Roman Catholic diocese of Oakland, California. She is a noted lecturer, author and editor in the areas of social ethics, theology in a global context and feminist/womanist theology. Her academic interests and expertise center around concerns related to the African American family.

H. Kathleen Hughes, RSCJ, PhD, is professor of word and worship at Catholic Theological Union in Chicago, Illinois. She is a member of the advisory boards of the International Commission on English in the Liturgy (ICEL) and the Bishops' Committee on the Liturgy. She is the author of *The Monk's Tale: A Biography of Godfrey Diekmann* (Liturgical Press, 1991); coeditor, with Joseph Favazza, of *Reconciliation Sourcebook* (Liturgy Training Publications, 1997); and author of numerous articles in scholarly and popular journals.

Robert J. Kennedy is assistant professor of liturgical studies and coordinator of student formation at Saint Bernard's Institute in Rochester, New York. In addition to the present volume, he is the editor of *Reconciliation: The Continuing Agenda* (Liturgical Press, 1987).

Margaret M. Mitchell, PhD, is associate professor of New Testament at McCormick Seminary in Chicago, Illinois. She is author of *Paul and the Rhetoric of Reconciliation: An Exegetical Investigation of the Language and Composition of 1 Corinthians* (Westminster/John Knox, 1993), and several articles, book reviews and scholarly papers on Pauline studies and John Chrysostom's use of Christian scriptures.

Paul J. Philibert, OP, STD, is director of the Institute for Church Life at the University of Notre Dame, a cluster for pastoral service in the United States in the areas of social justice, liturgical renewal, spirituality and continuing pastoral education. He has written on the nature and status of religious life since Vatican II, researched the relationship between moral education and spirituality, and has collaborated with noted liturgical artist Frank Kacmarcik on a book of basic Christian symbols, *Seeing and Believing* (Liturgical Press, 1995).

Fredric M. Roberts, PHD, is Associate Professor of Anthropology at Michigan State University in East Lansing, Michigan. His articles have appeared in several anthropological journals in the United States and abroad. He is coeditor with Nathan Mitchell of Liturgy Digest 2:2 (spring/summer 1995).